Welcoming the Other

 **McMaster Divinity College Press**
McMaster Studies in Practical Theology, Volume 2

The learning paradigm at McMaster Divinity College is summarized and guided by three deceptively simple words: Knowing, Being, Doing. In many senses, Knowing and Doing are significantly easier to qualify and quantify, while Being is notoriously elusive. Nonetheless, in practical theology—a discipline that is difficult to narrowly define but inevitably has something to do with what can be learned theologically and theoretically from our practice(s)—it is the study (Knowing) of our practice (Doing) that ultimately has an impact on who we are (Being) and how we relate to God. Many could argue that it is our practices and our approaches to practices (of ministry, of service, of reflection, to name a few) that both reveal and shape who we are. In this series, the McMaster Studies in Practical Theology, we offer space for those who are investigating practices that offer something to theology, even if they are not overtly theological, to publish significant work on this exciting and diverse discipline, and to draw on investigations and observations of practice(s) to contribute to the larger conversation and related fields of research. Recent graduates who have invested their academic research in this broad area are welcome to submit manuscripts for possible inclusion in the series, but we also invite both new and well-seasoned academic writers from around the world to submit their work for possible publication.

Welcoming the Other
An Ethnographic Study of Hospitality

J. Greg Sinclair

WIPF & STOCK · Eugene, Oregon

WELCOMING THE OTHER
An Ethnographic Study of Hospitality

McMaster Studies in Practical Theology, Volume 2
McMaster Divinity College Press

Copyright © 2025 J. Greg Sinclair. All rights reserved. Except for brief quotations in critical publications or reviews, no part of this book may be reproduced in any manner without prior written permission from the publisher. Write: Permissions, Wipf and Stock Publishers, 199 W. 8th Ave., Suite 3, Eugene, OR 97401.

Pickwick Publications
An Imprint of Wipf and Stock Publishers
199 W. 8th Ave., Suite 3
Eugene, OR 97401

McMaster Divinity College Press
1280 Main Street West
Hamilton, Ontario, L8S 4K1
Canada

www.wipfandstock.com

mcmasterdivinity.ca/mdcpress

PAPERBACK ISBN: 979-8-3852-5669-3
HARDCOVER ISBN: 979-8-3852-5670-9
EBOOK ISBN: 979-8-3852-5671-6

Cataloguing-in-Publication data:

Names: Sinclair, J. Greg, author

Title: Welcoming the other : a model for faith-based research / J. Greg Sinclair.

Description: Eugene, OR: Pickwick Publications, 2025 | McMaster Studies in Practical Theology | Includes bibliographical references.

Identifiers: ISBN 979-8-3852-5669-3 (paperback) | ISBN 979-8-3852-5670-9 (hardcover) | ISBN 979-8-3852-5671-6 (ebook)

Subjects: LCSH: Emigration and immigration. | Ethnography. | Hospitality--Religious Aspects

Classification: BR115.E45 S56 2025 (paperback) | BR115.E45 (ebook)

09/26/25

I dedicate this research project to the members of Willowdale Christian Reformed Church who showed me a vision of what the church in all her diversity and beauty can be.

Contents

List of Illustrations | ix
Acknowledgements | xi

Chapter 1
Introduction | 1

Chapter 2
Hospitality and Inclusion | 21

Chapter 3
Research Methodology | 53

Chapter 4
Discussion of Data | 71

Chapter 5
Theological Reflection | 112

Chapter 6
Concluding Thoughts | 160

Appendix
Ethnographic Research Interview Questions | 169

Bibliography | 173
Index of Modern Authors | 181
Index of Ancient Sources | 183

List of Illustrations

Figure 1: Prevalence of Domains | 74

Figure 2: Affective Domains | 86

Figure 3: Challenge Domains | 99

Acknowledgements

THIS RESEARCH PROJECT WOULD not have been possible without the support of my colleagues at Resonate Global Mission who supported my sabbatical and gave me space to pursue this research in practical theology. I also want to acknowledge the support of the council and members of Willowdale Christian Reformed Church, both English and Farsi-speaking Iranian members, who encouraged me to pursue this research project and welcomed me at their worship services. I also want to thank those who volunteered to be interviewed and for the support in sending out the letters of information.

During the research phase and the writing phases of this dissertation, I was part of a two peer student groups of doctoral students who gave me encouragement and shared insights from their own research experience. In several cases, they helped me to make wise decisions and avoid procedural errors in my qualitative study. I was shepherded well through the whole doctor of practical theology process by my supervisor Dr. Gordon Heath, and I am very grateful for his steady guidance. I am also grateful to my second reader Dr. Steve Studebaker. Dr. Sung Ho (Daniel) Ahn (external) and Dr. James Dvorak (Chairperson) rounded out my examination committee. I appreciate their good questions and sage advice.

Finally, I would like to thank my children for their support and for their love of learning, that I see evidence of daily, and for the support of my dear wife Nelly who has always encouraged me to keep learning and growing. Thank you.

Chapter 1

Introduction

EMERGING DIASPORA MINISTRY

IMAGES OF MIGRANTS JOURNEYING across the Mediterranean Sea in flimsy boats while others swim across the Colorado River at the US border are ubiquitous in the present day. Populations are in flux and migrating at unprecedented levels. Global migration affects the world in new and unprecedented ways. The focus of this study is the impact on global migration on the church in Canada today. The challenge for the church today is to be a welcoming community to these new Canadians. Iranians are part of this global diaspora, seeking a new start in a country with political stability and freedom of religion. Many Iranians settle in the Yonge Street corridor in Toronto, the setting where this case study occurred. Such diaspora communities need support to successfully transition to life in Canada. This is certainly true for Iranians who struggle with language issues and employment. Iranian believers that I know have shared with me that some Iranian students are unable to register until they become convention refugees and avoid the high cost of international student tuition. This is a call to the church to help these populations settle in Canada.

At the same time, the Protestant Church in Canada today faces numerical decline and the need to become ethnically diverse to reflect Canadian society. Reversing this decline and growing healthy congregations can happen through the welcome and inclusion of surrounding diaspora people groups and ethnic minority communities. An important aspect of missional outreach and including new ethnic minority communities is blending cultures. Such welcome and acceptance are increasingly important as Canadian society becomes less Christian and, as Lee Beach proposes, a post-Christian society.[1] This leads towards an exilic orientation for the church in Canada and a new missional orientation for the church. Such an exilic orientation aligns better with marginalized diaspora populations. The loss of Christendom brings the church closer to marginalized communities. Beach notes that living missionally will mean living in ways that open the church family to newcomers and strangers.[2]

Reginald Bibby notes in his book *Restless Gods* that, in the 1960s, "the Canadian religious roof had developed a noticeable leak."[3] This was the beginning of a decline in church attendance in Canada. Brian Clarke and Stuart Macdonald quantify this continuing leak noting that mainline Protestant denominations in Canada have declined from 9.9 million Canadians in 1981 to 8.7 million Canadians in 2011.[4] There is a specific note regarding the Christian Reformed Church's membership decline in the 1980s, due to controversy around women in leadership. The church in Canada is more polarized than ever and many Canadians are taking a pass on organized religion.[5] The church is still in demand but could do a better job of responding to people's religious needs.[6] Welcoming new groups such as the Persian community is a way to address diaspora people's needs and to bring new vibrancy to Canadian churches.

Diaspora focused ministry is an opportunity for the church to reach out to people with the good news of the gospel. Sam George of the Lausanne Diaspora Committee identifies the present refugee crisis as the "greatest humanitarian crisis of our time" and having "great potential" as many refugees come from highly religious cultures and

1. Beach, *Church in Exile*, 17.
2. Beach, *Church in Exile*, 199.
3. Bibby, *Restless Gods*, 12.
4. Clarke and Macdonald, *Leaving Christianity*, 69.
5. Bibby, *Beyond the Gods and Back*, 207.
6. Clark and Macdonald, *Leaving Christianity*, 230.

Introduction

have had dreams and visions drawing them to Christ. God seems to be drawing many refugees to himself.[7] This is a great missional opportunity for the church in Canada today.

J. D. Payne also sees the potential for diaspora focused ministry to share the gospel of salvation with diaspora people groups through missional outreach. Payne observes that the history of humanity is a history of migration.[8] Diaspora communities are part of God's plan for humanity, and God can use this present migration for his purposes. He writes:

> The Lord of the Harvest has been moving some of the world's unreached and least reached peoples to countries where governmental opposition will not interfere with missionary labors and where obtaining a visa and the costs of travel are not an issue. The church in the West must remember her missional nature and function intentionally, strategically, and apostolically.[9]

Newcomers to Canada come from countries that are closed to missionary work and so diaspora ministry presents new opportunities for mission outreach and support. Newcomers from Iran would fit this new reality as mission work in Iran is both limited and could even be dangerous.

Diaspora groups also bring gifts to the church in Canada. Rick Love outlines different cultural traits and worldviews in his book *Muslims, Magic and the Kingdom of God* where he notes the personal/spiritual worldview evident in folk Islam and the mechanistic/natural worldview more common in Western countries.[10] Such different worldviews make integrating Iranian believers into Canadian churches challenging, but the Iranian believers also bring gifts of recognizing the work of the Spirit.

Alan Roxburgh, in his examination of the Luke–Acts narrative, sees the importance of the language that Luke gives to the church at

---

7. George and Adeney, *Refugee Diaspora*, xix–xx.
8. Payne, *Strangers Next Door*, 29.
9. Payne, *Strangers Next Door*, 33.
10. Love, Muslims, *Magic and the Kingdom of God*, 75.

the end of the first century. The context in which Luke was writing was a period of change, when the original witnesses of the events of the gospels had died, and there was mounting pressure and persecution of Christians under the Roman authorities. Luke gives a new missional language to the church that is helpful to the modern church to go through change from dominance and power in the culture to a more marginalized position. This shift is helpful for leaving the language of colonial Christendom behind and moving to a place similar to the sent-out disciples in Luke 10. Now the missional narrative is about being a guest, about finding a person of peace, and about staying in one place and accepting hospitality. The good news of the gospel can be heard and absorbed in a place of mutual listening and learning.[11]

WILLOWDALE CRC (CHRISTIAN REFORMED CHURCH) CASE STUDY

Sometime around 2018, the pastor of Willowdale CRC in North York, Ontario, Canada—which I will refer to as WCRC from here on in—approached me to provide support to their growing Iranian community. I agreed and attended a meeting at the house of the pastor where about ten Iranian members of the Farsi Fellowship group of WCRC met for Bible study. I was impressed by their warm welcome and by their eagerness to study God's word. They also recounted episodes of persecution and trauma experienced due to their Christian faith in the country of Iran. The leaders continued to seek my support as part of my role supporting and encouraging missions among diaspora people groups with Resonate Global Mission, one of the mission agencies of the Christian Reformed Church of North America (CRCNA). Since that time, I have attended several Farsi Fellowship meetings and now teach and preach once per month on a Thursday evening. The enthusiasm of the Iranian community to learn from God's word continues and they always have interesting questions in the discussion time that happens post-sermon. The discussion, usually translated from English to Farsi and back to English by one of the Iranian leaders of the fellowship, ranges around a variety of topics related to living the Christian life. The focus on my

---

11. Roxburgh, *Missional*, 122–23.

Introduction

first sermon series was on the seven deadly sins tradition of virtue ethics. My second sermon series was on the Beatitudes. I had two opportunities to preach to the whole community of WCRC in English over the research period.

I also joined the board of Spiritual Growth Ministries, a separate charitable organization that is connected to WCRC to reach out to Farsi-speaking Iranians locally and globally. The leaders currently utilize social media to share information about biblical studies and other resources. They are also in the process of experimenting with an internet-based radio station with ongoing Christian programming in Farsi.

My focus for the last ten years has been on outreach to Muslim people groups, although over the last several years it has broadened to a focus on diaspora people groups in Canada and the US. With a huge number of diaspora people groups settling in Canada, there are new opportunities for ministry, as is evident in the experience of the Willowdale congregation and the changes that they have experienced over the last three years. WCRC has welcomed more than one hundred new Iranian believers since 2018 and regularly have ten to twenty baptisms. This is a unique situation in the Christian Reformed Church and the reason for this book project. My hope is that the knowledge and wisdom derived from this study will help other Christian Reformed churches. God is bringing to Canada people of different ethnic and cultural backgrounds.

Iranian (also called Persian) believers come from the country of Iran and are proud of their ancient history and of references in the Bible to the Persian Empire and kings such as Cyrus and Darius. They come from a society deeply influenced by *Shiite* Islam and by an authoritarian form of government since the Islamic revolution in 1979. I will use the terms "Persian" and "Iranian" interchangeably to reference this community. Another way to refer to this community is through their use of the Farsi language.

Members of the Christian Reformed Church in Canada mainly come from a Dutch background with many members having immigrated after World War II. Christian Reformed churches hold to a continental Reformed theological tradition influenced by John Calvin,

Herman Bavinck, and Abraham Kuyper. The church holds to three main confessions: the Heidelberg Catechism; the Belgic Confession; and the Canons of Dort. The church in general continues to diversify. WCRC exists in an urban Toronto context and so is more diverse than many CRCs in Canada. At present, about half of the attendees of WCRC are Farsi-speaking Iranians.[12] Although the focus of this book is on Iranian believers at WCRC, the congregation has other ethnic minority groups such as Korean and Filipino members.

The problem that I seek to address in this book is the lack of diversity in the Christian Reformed Church of North America (CRCNA) in Canada and the challenge of welcoming those who are very different culturally. This problem limits the possibilities for mission and for growing into ethnically diverse churches. In relation to this, my thesis is that there is an identifiable set of practices, rituals, or in other words, a *habitus*, around welcoming and being welcomed. These practices, rituals, and culture will be observed and analyzed through a qualitative methodology and reflected on theologically. Such reflection can in turn influence the practice of hospitality in a practice-reflection type of action reflection model. My aim is that ultimately this knowledge be shared with other congregations in Canada seeking to welcome their diverse neighbours. The WCRC community is a serendipitous opportunity to study such phenomena of welcome.

A QUALITATIVE APPROACH

John Swinton and Harriet Mowat note that situations "are complex, multifaceted entities which need to be examined with care, rigor and discernment if they are to be effectively understood."[13] Such complexity applies to the experience of welcome at WCRC between two very different cultures and traditions. Ward adds, in such situations of complexity, "Empirical research and particularly qualitative methods of inquiry are a means to explore situations in a more sustained and structured manner, offering multilayered and richly textured accounts

---

12. Westrate, "This is our Church."
13. Swinton and Mowat, *Practical Theology*, 15.

Introduction

of experience."[14] For this reason, a qualitative approach is most effective for research into this situation of cultural complexity.

As indicated by Nieman, a case study such as this in a congregational setting would benefit from an ethnographic approach. Ethnography "is a method for researching and understanding both the gaps and the connections between theology and lived faith practices."[15] Ethnography is especially helpful for studying the *habitus*, "the sum of the unspoken and yet firmly entrenched rules or patterns that govern the way a group of people practice their faith."[16] Thus, it is a good method for practice-led research. Such new knowledge "provides a basis for theological reflection and interpretation in light of the scriptures and the stated theologies of the group."[17] According to Moschella, an ethnography is "a form of pastoral listening that can analogously help a congregation or a community to find its collective voice."[18] The leaders of WCRC have expressed a desire to understand better their experience of welcoming the other, and being welcomed, and to reflect theologically on their experience.

Swinton and Mowat provide guidance in pursuing qualitative research that can provide accurate data in a congregational setting for further theological reflection. Qualitative research recognizes that human beings are constantly making sense of their world and their experiences through interpretative and meaning-seeking processes. Qualitative research involves identifying and understanding these meanings in the midst of the complexity of human life.[19] An initial step in qualitative research is developing a research question.[20] Moschella refers to Mason's four types of research puzzles, and this particular study would fall into the first example of a combination of a developmental puzzle and a mechanical puzzle asking "How did this come to

---

14. Ward, *Introducing Practical Theology*, 103.
15. Moschella, "Ethnography," 224.
16. Moschella, "Ethnography," 224.
17. Moschella, "Ethnography," 224.
18. Moschella, *Ethnography as a Pastoral Practice*, 13.
19. Swinton and Mowat, *Practical Theology*, 29.
20. Swinton and Mowat, *Practical Theology*, 50.

be and how is it maintained?"[21] The research question is: "How did it come to be that a Christian Reformed church welcomed one hundred and twenty Farsi-speaking Iranians into their congregation over a three year period, and how does that welcome unfold in the present and continue into the future?" It would be important to interview the members acting in the role of host as well as the Iranians as guests. Hospitality is a dynamic where both host and guest interact for mutual benefit. Guests, especially marginalized ones, are empowered when they are allowed to act as host.[22]

RESEARCH QUESTIONS

The research questions involved in this study revolve around understanding the church's response to this new reality of diaspora groups living in neighbourhoods around Christian Reformed churches like WCRC. As the congregation of WCRC has welcomed new Canadians from Iran, we can ask: What are some of the theological beliefs, practices and rituals that have developed in this congregational culture to allow them to welcome and include new Canadians from Iran? In other words, "How would we describe and understand the *habitus* of the congregation? How is the church presently practicing welcome and inclusion? What are some of the struggles that they have experienced? What are some of the breakthroughs of understanding and insights that they can share from their experience? Can we identify a culture of welcome? How do these practices compare and contrast between the two communities that make up the congregation? How has the Iranian community received hospitality and given hospitality back to their hosts?

THEORETICAL CONTRIBUTIONS

This book utilizes an ethnographic method of observation and interviews. James Spradley describes ethnography as "the work of describing a culture."[23] Spradley notes that ethnography is not studying people

---

21. Moschella, *Ethnography as a Pastoral Practice*, 64.
22. Pohl, *Making Room*, 121.
23. Spradley, *Ethnographic Interview*, 3.

but learning from people in order to understand their point of view.[24] One theoretical aspect of ethnographic research through interviewing informants is the relational theory of meaning. This theory includes "decoding cultural symbols and the underlying coding rules."[25] This theory states that language, through interviewing informants in a particular culture, will help to understand the culture, both through the identification of symbols and through the relationships of those symbols within a specific culture. The only way for someone outside of a cultural system to understand the practices, rituals, and shared implicit knowledge is to use language symbols and codes to give insight into the bigger system of hospitality at work in the congregation. This can be difficult in a system that appears like other systems. In my case, I am familiar with Christian Reformed congregations. Each congregation is different, and yet congregations have common aspects such as the order of worship. Although Christian Reformed churches continue to diversify in terms of their worship, it is important that I do not assume that I know the culture or the practices but rather derive this knowledge through noting symbols and codes unique to this congregation. Such an approach allows the ethnographer to understand the culture and experience of the informants through analyzing these symbols. Using Spradley's method of domain analysis and taxonomic analysis has allowed me to understand the experience of hospitality and welcome from the experience of the informants. This method of analysis also allowed me to understand their experience from their perspective, while at the same time limiting the addition of my own perspective.

Two theories of social contact relate to the mixing of two different cultures under the rubric of intergroup contact and are useful for examining and understanding hospitality in a church setting from a social psychological perspective. Those theories are intergroup contact theory and social identity theory (and the related self-categorization theory). Social identity theory involves reducing human diversity to a limited set of categories in order to cope with complexity.[26] Henri Tajfel observes that "an individual strives to achieve a satisfactory concept

---

24. Spradley, *Ethnographic Interview*, 3.
25. Spradley, *Ethnographic Interview*, 99.
26. Hinton, *Perception of People*, 55.

or image of himself."²⁷ This image or self-concept is derived from a social group and the comparison between social groups.²⁸ This leads to categorization of others, which in turn accentuates group differences.²⁹ Contact theory includes the idea that people become more familiar and comfortable with others through contact. Gordon Allport points out that in the Detroit riot of 1943, neighbours did not riot against each other.³⁰ Allport concluded that "prejudice may be reduced by equal status contact between majority and minority groups in the pursuit of common goals."³¹ Vezzali and Stathi, in reflecting on Allport's work, state, "contact between individuals who belong to different groups can foster the development of more positive out-group attitudes."³² Contact can therefore lead to a change in social identity and reduce the tendency to categorize others as "other." Through observation and interviews, I evaluate how much these theories of social contact and identity are evident in the WCRC community in order to reflect theologically on intergroup contact in the church today.

THEOLOGICAL FRAMEWORKS

Data will be analyzed, both from observation of the WCRC community and through informant interviews. This analysis will lead to theological reflection on the identified beliefs and practices to help the congregation better understand their culture and context and to continue to grow in their welcome and inclusion of Persians and other diaspora people groups. The main method of theological reflection in this book will be a linear applied reflection, which matches the experience of the congregation with Scripture passages and reflection from theologians. Ballard and Pritchard note that this is the most basic method of theological reflection connecting the situation under review to biblical wisdom and authority. Other sources such as the teaching of the church

27. Tajfel, *Human Groups and Social Categories*, 254.
28. Tajfel, *Human Groups and Social Categories*, 255.
29. Hinton, *Perception of People*, 55.
30. Allport, *Nature of Prejudice*, 250.
31. Allport, *Nature of Prejudice*, 267.
32. Vezzali and Stathi, "Present and the Future of the Contact Hypothesis," 1.

Introduction

and systematic theology may be used.[33] Where sociological reflection occurs, a correlation methodology is used. Correlational methods are helpful with theological conversation partners in the human sciences.[34]

Jesus' redemptive work on the cross makes inclusion possible. Jesus as the new Adam brings healing to creation and to human society and culture. It is through Jesus that diverse people can come together in community. Louis Berkhof points to the importance in Reformed theological thinking of humanity as created in the image of God and humans as God-related.[35] This God imaging quality ties humanity together and indicates that the default stance towards others is respect and solidarity. The divine image also provides a theological foundation for community formation and inclusion of cultural diversity. Reformed theology has made a place for welcoming the stranger. John Calvin welcomed refugees into his city of Geneva and encouraged the churches to be welcoming.[36] Calvin also encouraged the stewarding of material gifts and the distribution to the neighbour's benefit.[37] Such a stance is important in intercultural ministry. Robert Cousins, in examining intercultural ministry, writes of God's missional mandate to bless the nations.[38] The gospel leads to the restoration of the true order of values, though the power of sin is great.[39]

Another important aspect of a theology of welcome is recognition. Concerning the power of recognition, Christine Pohl writes, "recognition involves respecting the dignity and worth of every person and valuing their contributions, to the larger community."[40] Recognition begins with recognizing Jesus in the stranger (Matt 25). Recognizing Jesus in the stranger gives them dignity and worth and a warm welcome. The other part of recognition is the "two-way street" role of

---

33. Ballard and Pritchard, *Practical Theology in Action*, 129.
34. Ballard and Pritchard, *Practical Theology in Action*, 131.
35. Berkhof, *Systematic Theology*, 202.
36. Lee, "What John Calvin Taught (Me)."
37. Calvin, *Institutes* 3.7.5.
38. Cousins, "Blessed to Be a Blessing," 45.
39. Niebuhr, *Christ and Culture*, 53.
40. Pohl, *Making Room*, 61.

hospitality. The host is blessed by the guest, the guest by the host, and together they realize that both are helping each other in mutuality.[41]

Invitation and inclusion are other important aspects of a theology of welcome. Roy Oksnevad, in *The Burden of Baggage*, notes that, in interviews with Farsi-speaking Iranians, some felt they could benefit from integration into existing North American English-speaking churches.[42] Miroslav Volf sees the path to inclusion and embrace as beginning in the Trinitarian nature of God where the members of the Trinity have co-inherence, a mutual interiority or *perichoresis* that exhibits a beautiful reciprocity.[43] Volf's approach of embrace and re-embrace as a kind of dance of welcoming the other is a helpful theology for including Farsi-speaking Iranians into established congregations in Canada.

Sandra Van Opstal writes in the context of worship leadership of the importance of this reciprocity. It is not enough just to welcome some people of different ethnicities and cultures onto the worship team. This can result in mere tokenism. It is important to allow them to lead from their own cultural background. This involves listening and understanding—which Van Opstal refers to as solidarity—and then, in time, really needing the other, which Van Opstal calls mutuality.[44] A theology of welcome not only includes initial contact with a new group but also inclusion and mutuality of ongoing relationship.

A theology of welcome begins with God's gracious welcome to sinners through Jesus Christ. It includes the historic welcome of groups into the church including Calvin's work with refugees in Geneva. It works against sin, fear, tribalism, and exclusion to embrace the other through inclusion, recognition, and mutual acceptance. It is a work of God and a work of grace in the life of a congregation.

Amos Yong points out that the Holy Spirit helps the church to faithfully improvise the twenty-ninth chapter of Acts in "times and places far removed from Theophilus' original situation."[45] He goes on

---

41. Pohl, *Making Room*, 72.
42. Oksnevad, *Burden of Baggage*, 31.
43. Volf, *Exclusion and Embrace*, 128.
44. Van Opstal, *Next Worship*, 75.
45. Yong, *Hospitality and the Other*, 55.

Introduction

to argue that the Spirit is at work in the practices of the church.[46] God as Trinity—Father, Son, and Holy Spirit—is at work in the story of WCRC and the changing congregation. Yong notes that certain virtues such as openness, humility, and understanding arise from the Spirit and help God's word to be interpreted and practiced.[47] In an increasingly pluralistic society, many languages, discourses, and tongues "are the means through which Christian witness is borne and the salvation of the world is effected."[48]

Christian Scharen and Aana Marie Vigen note that ethnography is a way to focus on the particular to "discover truth revealed through embodied habits, relations, practices, narratives and struggles."[49] This leads to their conviction that each life, situation, or community "is potentially, albeit only partially, revelatory of transcendent or divine truth."[50] This leads them to conclude that ethnography is a form of embodied theology. The analysis of the ethnographic research will lead to further reflection on this embodied theology of welcoming that will in turn affect the practice of this congregation and other congregations in Canada.

METHODOLOGY

The methodology for this book is a qualitative ethnographic study of an established congregation welcoming a minority ethnic group. This research project studies the culture of both the long-term members of a Dutch Canadian background and the new Persian members. Over a period from January 15 to March 31, 2022, I observed the congregation in two settings on a weekly basis, and I interviewed four host culture members and five new Persian culture members and compared their experiences. I followed Spradley's ethnographic method (called the Developmental Research Sequence) to discover tacit and explicit cultural themes that are active in the culture of WCRC.[51]

46. Yong, *Hospitality and the Other*, 55.
47. Yong, *Hospitality and the Other*, 56.
48. Yong, *Hospitality and the Other*, 64.
49. Scharen and Vigen, "Preface," xxi.
50. Scharen and Vigen, "Preface," xxi.
51. Spradley, *Ethnographic Interview*, 134.

Spradley recommends intermixing descriptive, structural, and contrasting interview questions in a series of three interviews to understand both general themes as well as more in-depth analysis of a few specific themes in a population.[52] The interview questions use this methodology in an open-ended interview format. Translation was needed with one Farsi speaking informant and a translator from outside the community translated from English to Farsi and Farsi to English.

LIMITATIONS

The study for this book took place in the second year of the COVID-19 pandemic during the phase marked by the Omicron variant. This meant that interviews were on Zoom, and initial participant observation was on Zoom. Towards the end of the study, I was able to attend the Sunday morning service four times in person. Farsi Fellowship meetings, however, continued on Zoom. Church activities and social events were severely curtailed due to COVID-19 restrictions. Where possible, I noted pre-COVID references to hospitality and present adaptations to the restrictions.

A second limitation of this study is the small sample size. The small number of informants allowed for more than one interview from each informant to further identify and define cultural domains and understand specific practices and rituals. Despite the small number, it is possible to understand more fully the practices, ritual, and culture through Spradley's method, as opposed to a larger sample size of just one interview per informant. The focus of this research method, as in other qualitative studies, was not so much on many informants often associated with quantitative methods. Rather, it was to reach saturation of knowledge of the cultural situation. I identified informants through a general request from the church administrator to the members of the church. Participants then contacted me by email if they were interested in participating in the study. I am a member of the dominant white community (although not of Dutch ethnic heritage). I have consulted with the leadership council of WCRC, including the Iranian leaders

---

52. Spradley, *Ethnographic Interview*, 134.

Introduction

of the Farsi Fellowship, and they have been supportive of the project throughout. Moschella notes the importance of informed consent in an ethnographic study with human subjects.[53] Guidelines around consent for both the observation and interview components was explained through an announcement to the congregation, email scripts, and letters of information. For the observation component, an "opt out" option was given to members of the congregation as advised by the McMaster Research Ethics Board.[54] If a member was not comfortable with participating for whatever reason, they could contact a member of the council. Once advised of such a request, I did not take any notes referring to this individual. For the interviews, I used an oral consent script and recorded verbal consent into an oral consent log. The participants were de-identified through codes and anonymity was protected through the use of pseudonyms. I alerted the informants to the possibility of eventually publishing the data related to this research.[55]

As this research project has focused on one congregation and context, this book involves "an organized and systematic way of studying and reporting various aspects of a person, family, group, or situation utilizing a structured outline of subjects and questions."[56] Theological reflection arises out of the embodied theology in the rituals and practices and the culture of welcome of the congregation under study. The results identify new learnings and challenges that will lead to further theological reflection by the leaders of WCRC, as well as other congregations in the Christian Reformed denomination.[57] One of the limits of a case study like this is the difficulty of generalizing from one case to the next.[58] The advantage of a case study is that is has the potential of epistemic value that could generate new knowledge about welcoming the other.[59] This research project involves a congregation. The advantage of congregational studies is that they are well suited as a practical

---

53. Moschella, *Ethnography as a Pastoral Practice*, 88.
54. See "McMaster Research Ethics Board (MREB)."
55. Moschella, *Ethnography as a Pastoral Practice*, 97.
56. Shipani, "Case Study Method," 91.
57. Shipani, "Case Study Method," 98.
58. Shipani, "Case Study Method," 99.
59. Shipani, "Case Study Method," 96.

theological exercise of looking at human practices and rituals that may coalesce around complex domains of behaviour in order to convey hospitality, the practice in question for this book.[60]

REFLEXIVITY

Ethnographic research with informants lends itself to a post-modern hermeneutic that encourages attentiveness to the possibility of interpreter bias. It is important for the researcher to consider personal reflexivity, which considers all research to be autobiography.[61] Decisions must be made on what to include and exclude. The creation of identities and categories also exclude or include.[62] The researcher is inserted into a specific context with specific relationships of power and competition. Much attention must be paid to how one "thinks about thinking."[63] This necessitates the need for reflective research. Reflective research involves careful interpretation and reflection.[64] The first observation means that all references to empirical data are the results of interpretation.[65] The second observation is that reflection "turns attention 'inwards' towards the person of the researcher, the relevant research community, society as a whole, intellectual and cultural traditions, and the central importance, as well as the problematic nature of language and narrative (the form of presentation) in the research context." [66] Alvesson and Sköldberg note that it is difficult, if not impossible, for "researchers to clarify the taken for granted assumptions and blind spots in their own social culture, research community and language."[67]

For these reasons, I continue to reflect on my own personal journey that has led to this kind of research as an important exercise in reflexivity. I have worked in a cross-cultural Islamic context in West Africa for nine years and have pastored a Christian Reformed church

---

60. Nieman, "Congregational Studies," 140.
61. Swinton and Mowat, *Practical Theology*, 57.
62. Alvesson and Sköldberg, *Reflexive Methodology*, 264–65.
63. Alvesson and Sköldberg, *Reflexive Methodology*, 10.
64. Alvesson and Sköldberg, *Reflexive Methodology*, 11.
65. Alvesson and Sköldberg, *Reflexive Methodology*, 11.
66. Alvesson and Sköldberg, *Reflexive Methodology*, 11.
67. Alvesson and Sköldberg, *Reflexive Methodology*, 11.

Introduction

in Alberta for six years. This experience has given me experience in cross-cultural dynamics. Throughout the study period, I continually recorded observations in a journal as recommended by Moschella. The researcher "may be able to achieve a deeper and genuine understanding of the ethnographic encounter, their own role in it, and the 'shared wisdom' that may emerge from it."[68]

Such reflexivity includes a narrative of how God has worked in my life and brought me to this research project. I first became interested in global culture, and more particular in African culture, watching a movie about the South African journalist and anti-apartheid activist Steve Biko. Sometime later, newly married and living in Quebec, my wife and I befriended Wycliffe Bible translators preparing for service as linguists in West Africa. This led to discussions with Christian Reformed World Missions resulting first in a three-month experience in Mali with a summer missions program and then over eight years in Mali, West Africa, as a church developer working among the Fulani (Fulbe) people in various areas of the country. Most of our ministry occurred in the village of Yuvaru, located on the edge of the Niger River inland delta south of Timbuktu. This area of the Sahel region encompasses a large flood plain that produces fertile grazing land for the pastoralist Fulani people. Living in this isolated area, my family and I became dependent on Fulani neighbours for cultural knowledge and practice.

The strategy of our mission team involved a contextualized approach so that the gospel would speak into Fulani culture and not appear alien or Western. The goal was to allow the Holy Spirit to inform new Fulani believers of the small emerging church to develop practices and rituals that would fit naturally into Fulani culture. Where possible, new believers from an Islamic background were encouraged to pursue an insider approach and remain in their Islamic context even after becoming believers until they felt that they could be more open about their decision to follow Christ. This experience led me to be very comfortable in cross-cultural ministry settings and in working with people of other cultures and ethnicities. Working in the folk Islamic context of West Africa allowed me to understand Islamic theology with an underlay of animistic religion. I also read the Quran to understand

---

68. Moschella, *Ethnography as a Pastoral Practice*, 105.

Islamic practice and ritual. Many of the Fulani in my village followed a Sufi sect of Islam that involved mystical practices of healing and care through *Marabouts*, local practitioners of folk Islam. A number of Fulani males spent some time in Quranic schools and could read some Arabic. This experience informs my present ministry of working with diaspora populations in Canada and the US. This exposure to different types of Islamic experience has also been helpful in understanding the conversion experience of Iranian believers from an Islamic (*Shiite*) background and some of the cultural and theological challenges of conversion and discipleship faced by these new believers.

I also served for six years as a pastor of a Christian Reformed Church congregation in rural Alberta, Canada. This gave me insights into the Christian Reformed/Dutch Canadian subculture as well as values, practices, and traditions that are important to Christian Reformed people. One example of this is singing the song *Ere Zij God* on a yearly basis, usually at either Christmas or New Years. Many older CRC people remember singing this song as children and youth during the World War II years in the Netherlands. Older church members have vivid memories of surviving the war and immigrating to Canada. These two very different pastoral experiences help me as a researcher to be a bridge between Christian Reformed churches and other cultural groups. This also sometimes leads to my frustration when CRCNA congregations do not welcome other cultural groups and tend to be blind to prejudice and privilege. This could affect my interpretative process in undertaking research of this nature. I am thankful for the different experiences that provide a way to bridge different cultures and encourage diversity in the Christian Reformed Church. Tim Wise, in his book *White like Me*, refers to his own compelling interest in race and racism when he writes, "But for me, ignoring race and racism has never been an option. Even when it would have been easier to turn away, there were too many forces and circumstances pulling me back, compelling me to look at the matter square in the face—my face."[69] I feel the same way about cross-cultural ministry and helping the church to be a more diverse family of many cultures, races, and ethnic backgrounds. It is for this reason that this book is concerned with welcoming Persians at

---

69. Wise, *White like Me*, xii.

Introduction

this particular time, as God is bringing many in the Iranian diaspora to follow Jesus. How can we in the Christian Reformed Church open our arms to embrace them?

CHAPTER SUMMARY

Chapter 2: Hospitality and Inclusion

I explore the theme of hospitality. Themes related to hospitality include the following: recognition of the other; valuing the other as made in the image of God; seeing Christ in the stranger; appreciating God's plan for diversity; the role of host and guest and mutuality between the two; the theory of social contact and identity; the call to be missional; care for the refugee; and the work of God in bringing two very different cultures together.

Chapter 3: Research Methodology

I use James Spradley's Developmental Research Sequence Method to understand the congregational culture. I observed the congregation over a two-and-one-half-month period and interviewed nine informants, four from the host culture and five from the guest culture. The informants responded to a recruitment email. I gathered data through an ethnographic method of open-ended interviews with descriptive, structural, and contrasting questions. These questions and the subsequent analysis allowed me to understand the inputs and meanings behind the cultural domains expressed in the interviews.

Chapter 4: Discussion of Data

Data was coded using MaxQDA software and domains and sub-domains were identified. I then applied the data to understanding the practices and rituals (*habitus*) of welcoming in the church and emerging theories of welcoming diaspora populations into established churches. The study gives new insights into hospitality as two distinct communities come together in a congregation and the social contact dynamics of such an event. Reducing prejudice towards the other through increased contact and recognition of the other is an important part of welcoming the other and this is particularly true for Christian Reformed churches welcoming Persian believers.

Chapter 5: Theological Reflection

I reflect theologically on the data derived from the developmental sequence method as well as observation notes in an action-reflection cycle. This links the reflection directly to the *habitus* of welcoming as attributed to the informants and the practices of the congregation. This *habitus* is applied in a linear fashion to Scripture and theological thinking around welcoming the other. This embodied theology and reflection then sheds light on what God is doing in the context of WCRC and how the congregation can continue to reflect on this journey. Such a journey is only possible through God's grace and the continued help of the Holy Spirit in the continuing faithful improvisation and practice of God's mission. Amid complexity, such reflection helps to sustain and develop the communal life of the newly diverse congregation.

Chapter 6: Concluding Thoughts

This chapter concludes the study by reviewing the research problem of welcoming diaspora populations into established congregations and the thesis that WCRC exhibits a *habitus* of welcoming the stranger that is observable through participation and interviews with informants from the congregation. I summarize key findings of the research into welcoming the other from a different cultural and ethnic background with the emphasis on emergent understanding. Such insight has ramifications for the field of welcoming the other into established churches in Canada. Limitations of the study and areas for future research are identified.

Chapter 2

Hospitality and Inclusion

Hospitality as a practice has a long history in the Christian tradition. Hospitality can become a *habitus*. One focus that arose in this study is the importance of sacramental hospitality. I will give this some attention in reflecting on the importance of the Lord's Supper and baptism in the welcome of the other. I also hope to include thoughts on how hospitality leads to long term inclusion of the guest and the dance of the guest and the host in the movement of hospitality. In practical theology, often a social science conversation partner is helpful for understanding situations in all their complexity. I will consider some social theories around contact and identity that give further insights to two very cultural groups coming together to form a unified congregation.

There is a lack of examples in the current literature of churches welcoming the other from different cultural and ethnic backgrounds in the Canadian context. I have not found examples of churches in Canada welcoming Persian neighbours. The lack of examples in the Canadian context points to the necessity of this research project and the potential to contribute new information to an embodied theology of welcoming the other.

Welcoming the Other

Biblical and Theological Foundations of Hospitality

History of Hospitality

As we examine the history of Christian hospitality, two major themes emerge; receiving Christ in the stranger and seeing in the stranger God's image that ties together all of humanity. Christine Pohl notes that hospitality developed as a distinct Christian tradition in the early church, in continuity with Hebrew understanding of hospitality and in contrast to Hellenistic practices.[1] Such practices came to embrace the marginalized and those who could not reciprocate as the true recipients of hospitality.[2] This also meant the opposite was true, "to entertain persons who had few needs was not really hospitality at all."[3] Writers in the early church often referred to hospitality to the stranger as if one was receiving Christ himself. This reflects Jesus' teaching in Matt 25:31–46 where he identifies with the stranger who is hungry, thirsty, in need of shelter, clothing, is sick, or in prison. There is a wide concurrence in early Christian thought that, when we welcome the stranger who is in need, we are welcoming Christ.

The church father Ambrose writes, in *On Duties of the Clergy* (*De officiis ministrorum*), "how do you know that when you receive someone, you do not receive Christ? Christ may be in the stranger that comes, for Christ is there in the person of the poor as He himself says 'I was in prison and you came to me. I was naked and you clothed me.'"[4] In a similar vein, John Chrysostom often included the theme of hospitality in his homilies. He emphasizes that the one who receives a guest receives Christ in his *Homily 45 on the Acts of the Apostles* (*Homiliae in Acta apostolorum*): "Therefore too the one that receives Christ, shall receive the reward of whoever has Christ for a guest."[5] In his *Homily 21 on Romans* (*Homiliae in epistulam ad Romanos*), Chrysostom references

---

1. Pohl, *Making Room*, 17.
2. Pohl, *Making Room*, 17.
3. Pohl, *Making Room*, 19.
4. Oden, ed., *And You Welcomed Me*, 60.
5. Oden, ed., *And You Welcomed Me*, 61.

Abraham in encouraging his listeners not to be too curious about their guests. He writes, "Don't be curious then, either, since for Christ you receive him."[6] Thus, there is a sense in his homilies of welcoming Christ in the stranger and welcoming the stranger for Christ. He writes, in *Homily 14 on First Timothy* (*Homiliae in epistulam i ad Timotheum*), "If you receive the stranger as Christ, be not ashamed, but rather glory. But if you receive him not as Christ, receive him not at all."[7] Chrysostom also writes, in his *Homily 45 on the Acts of the Apostles*, "Let our house be Christ's general receiving place. Let us demand of them as a reward, not money, but that they make our house the receiving place for Christ."[8] For Chrysostom, the stranger is honoured as if Christ himself was present. Christine Pohl notes that for Chrysostom, hospitality was to be "offered personally, with one's own hands, not left exclusively for the church to provide."[9]

Amy Oden quotes Pseudo-Clementine from the early 200s as following: "If therefore you wish truly to honor the image of God, we declare to you what is true, that you should do good to, and pay honor and reverence to everyone, who is made in the image of God."[10] Welcoming the Persian *other* into Christian Reformed churches involves the creational truth that all people are created according to God's image. Genesis 1:27 says that God made the man and the woman in his own image. This ties all of humanity together despite very different historical, political, and cultural backgrounds. We begin with this foundational truth and always welcome the other as an image bearer of God. Soong-Chan Rah sees this passage from Genesis as an important protection against racism because racism elevates the physical image above the spiritual image. It is a turning away from God to the creature.[11] He goes on to write, "if we realize that all of humanity is created in the spiritual image of God and that there is a base equality in humanity's worth derived from God's image as well as humanity's tragedy

---

6. Oden, ed., *And You Welcomed Me*, 63.
7. Oden, ed., *And You Welcomed Me*, 64.
8. Oden, ed., *And You Welcomed Me*, 115.
9. Pohl, *Making Room*, 46.
10. Oden, ed., *And You Welcomed Me*, 54.
11. Rah, *Next Evangelicalism*, 81.

as fallen beings, then there would be no sense in asserting the superiority of one race over another.¹² For Rah, this passage is important for developing a multiethnic evangelicalism.

Paul Hartog explores similarities and influences in First Clement with Hebrews around the theme of hospitality. Abraham is praised for his "faith and hospitality," Lot for his "hospitality and godliness," and "hospitable" Rahab for receiving the Israelite spies.¹³ First Clement follows the order found in Hebrews for Old Testament examples of hospitality, Enoch, Noah, Abraham, Lot, and Rahab, although Hartog notes that this may also reflect the ordering of redemptive history.¹⁴ Abraham is in particular an interesting Old Testament example of hospitality as he was a sojourner in need of hospitality yet also a host extending hospitality. Hebrews references the possibility of receiving angels in reference to Abraham's experience in Gen 18. In both First Clement and Hebrews, faith is tied closely to hospitality of these Old Testament figures.¹⁵

Saint Francis of Assisi is a model of hospitality towards the other, particularly the *Muslim other*. Saint Francis traveled to dialogue with the Sultan Malik Al-Kamil in the midst of the Fifth Crusade. While there is some disagreement as to whether Saint Francis's approach was irenic or confrontational, it is true that in the midst of a war and call to Crusade by church leaders, Francis sought to dialogue with a Muslim leader. In *Earlier Rule* (*Regular non bullata*), Francis writes of missionary work among the Saracens and encourages his friars to avoid quarrels and disputes and to be subject to every human creature for God's sake so that they could bear witness to the fact that they are Christians.¹⁶ In their encounter, the Sultan "admired Francis's character, his whole hearted commitment to his faith and his clear contempt for the luxuries of the world."¹⁷ James De Vitry notes that the Sultan received

---

12. Rah, *Next Evangelicalism*, 82–83.
13. Hartog, "Abraham and the Rhetoric of Hospitality," 285.
14. Hartog, "Abraham and the Rhetoric of Hospitality," 286.
15. Hartog, "Abraham and the Rhetoric of Hospitality," 293.
16. Habig, *St. Francis of Assisi*, 43
17. Spoto, *Reluctant Saint*, 161.

Francis in a kindly way and dismissed him with honour.[18] Francis is a good example of hospitality received and extended while bearing a loving witness to the religious other.

In the Reformation period, John Calvin welcomed refugees into his city of Geneva and encouraged the churches to be welcoming. Moses Lee notes that Calvin was a refugee himself, and that he encouraged the churches to accept religious refugees, even disciplining native Genevans for "public xenophobic outbursts."[19] In his *Institutes of the Christian Religion*, Calvin encourages Christians to "renounce yourself and give yourself wholly to others."[20] Calvin also encouraged the stewarding of material gifts and the distribution to the neighbour's benefit.[21] Pohl notes that, for Calvin, welcoming Protestant refugees fleeing persecution was a "most sacred kind of hospitality."[22] Galatians 3:28–29 points as well to the work of the Spirit in bringing down dividing walls of hostility between men and women, Jew and Greek, and slave and free. This is an important passage in integrating people of different cultures and ethnicities. If you are Abraham's seed, then you are heirs of the kingdom according to the promise made to Abraham of imputed righteousness through Christ. This then unifies all believers in the church in their diversity. John Calvin, in his commentary on Galatians, states, "The meaning is, that there is no distinctions of persons here, and therefore it is of no consequence to what nation or condition anyone may belong: nor is circumcision any more than sex or civil rank. And why? Because Christ makes them all one."[23]

However, in contrast to Calvin's attitude towards refugees, the Reformation period also saw a change from a sacramental idea of hospitality (welcoming Christ in the stranger) as reflected in Chrysostom, to a more civic and domestic duty. This was especially true for Luther who saw hospitality as "an act of obedience, a practical response

---

18. Almedingen, *St. Francis of Assisi*, 145.
19. Lee, "What John Calvin Taught (Me)."
20. Calvin, *Institutes* 3.7.5.
21. Calvin, *Institutes* 3.7.5.
22. Pohl, *Making Room*, 52.
23. Calvin, *Commentary on the Epistles of Paul to the Galatians and Ephesians*, 112.

to human need."²⁴ Pohl reflects that this move towards the domestic and civic spheres has contributed to hospitality's detachment from its Christian roots as it became increasingly secularized.²⁵ That is why in our modern era, hospitality is more often associated with hotels and restaurants than people's homes.

In contemporary times, Robert Cousins, in examining intercultural ministry, writes that God's missional mandate to bless the nations will "require God's people to cross cultural boundaries to build trusting relations for the sharing of the gospel."²⁶ The gospel leads to the restoration of the true order of values, though the power of sin is great.²⁷ It is through Jesus that diverse people can come together in community and be welcomed, recognized, become friends, be discipled, and feel needed. It is through the inclusivity of Christ's work that community is shaped, shame and honour issues are resolved, forgiveness is experienced, trauma healed, and racism is overcome.

Moving into the present, I will now examine some important themes related to hospitality, welcoming the other, and specifically welcoming refugees who are newcomers to Canada from Iran. What are the relevant issues for church leaders to continue in welcoming the stranger from other ethnic groups and cultures and what are the challenges specific to the Iranian community? This involves thinking about friendship, being both host and guest, recognition, discipleship, and inclusion. Let us start by thinking about what it means to welcome the stranger.

Welcoming the Stranger

Is the stranger a friend or an enemy? Ross Langmead notes that the New Testament word for stranger (*xenos*) means both guest and host, and our response to the stranger dictates whether they remain a stranger or become a guest.²⁸ Langmead defines hospitality as a stronger term than we currently understand, utilizing the "strong and multidimensional

---

24. Pohl, *Making Room*, 53.
25. Pohl, *Making Room*, 53.
26. Cousins, "Blessed to Be a Blessing," 45.
27. Niebuhr, *Christ and Culture*, 53.
28. Langmead, "Refugees as Guests and Hosts," 36.

concept similar to public friendship in classical Greek times which (although only available between peers) involved solidarity and defense of the other."[29] Langmead sees hospitality resulting from divine action, as a response to God's "gifting and honoring human beings with the super abundant hospitality of God."[30] Mission and hospitality are tied together as responses to God's good news of the gospel. Langmead contrasts mission as a centrifugal force and as centripetal force. The world coming to the Western church through migration is the centripetal correction to the centrifugal force of earlier mission efforts. Such balance brings new opportunities for mutuality and transformation of both host and guest.[31] Such hospitality also brings us into areas of justice work such as advocacy, human rights, settlement issues, and sanctuary. Langmead observes, "Jesus constantly broke boundaries and reversed the social order in affirming the human dignity and blessedness of those on the margins of this society—the women, children, ritually impure, poor, sick, cultural outsiders and moral failures."[32] Jesus' message is relevant to refugees on the margins because it is "good news for those who are persecuted as justice seekers (Matt 5:10) and for those who are poor, who weep now and are hungry (Luke 6:21)."[33] Langmead notes that Jesus centred himself in a rich Hebrew tradition of God's mercy and justice. God is a "refuge for the oppressed, a place of safety in times of trouble (Ps 9:9)."[34]

Radical hospitality arises from Jesus' proclamation in Luke 4:18–19 that he was sent by God to bring good news to the poor, the captives, the blind and the oppressed, which he linked to the prophet Isaiah (Isa 61:1–2). Jaeyeon Lucy Chung advocates for a pastoral theology based on radical hospitality towards the marginalized Asian American community that is undocumented and does not fit the "model immigrant" stereotype that had developed around Asian Americans.[35] Radical

29. Langmead, "Refugees as Guests and Hosts," 37.
30. Langmead, "Refugees as Guests and Hosts," 37.
31. Langmead, "Refugees as Guests and Hosts," 38.
32. Langmead, "Refugees as Guests and Hosts," 34.
33. Langmead, "Refugees as Guests and Hosts," 35.
34. Langmead, "Refugees as Guests and Hosts," 35.
35. Chung, "Toward an Asian American Pastoral Theology," 128.

hospitality has the potential to reduce barriers and transform the entire community.[36]

Pierre-Francois de Bethune points out that the etymology of the words "host" and "guest" are from the same Indo-European root *ghos-ti* where the words for hospitality and hostility are derived.[37] Such etymology implies that the guest can be both friend and enemy and it is possible that the tradition of hospitality weighed this balance—it is better to treat the stranger carefully. De Bethune observes that the act of hospitality can lead one to willingness to "love one's enemy."[38] The key to hospitality is honouring the stranger while not assimilating the stranger—hospitality is about honouring the difference yet also transcending it.

Hospitality has a lot of potential for reflection through a theological action–reflection cycle. Such theological reflection could lead to new knowledge that informs continuing practice for the congregation and for other congregations while allowing for limitations in generalizing within the case study method. Ward notes that reflection involves "a survey of the key theological literature and also the empirical literature that relates to the designated problem."[39] Practical theological research is about lived religion, and so an ethnographic approach to this kind of research is helpful. This means that the researcher must pay close attention to "the experiences of ordinary believers and how they live their lives in relation to religion."[40] Sometimes this leads to hybridity which Ward defines as a mixture of different and even contradictory perspectives."[41]

Henri Nouwen emphasizes the movement from hostility to hospitality. He writes that hostility is converted into hospitality when "fearful strangers can become guests revealing to their hosts the promise they are carrying with them."[42] Nouwen references both the three visitors

---

36. Chung, "Toward an Asian American Pastoral Theology," 129.
37. de Bethune, *Interreligious Hospitality*, 118.
38. de Bethune, *Interreligious Hospitality*, 118.
39. Ward, *Introducing Practical Theology*, 100.
40. Ward, *Introducing Practical Theology*, 57.
41. Ward, *Introducing Practical Theology*, 57.
42. Nouwen, *Reaching Out*, 67.

that Abraham hosted (Gen 18:1–15) and the travelers on the road to Emmaus (Luke 24:13–35). Guests carry precious gifts with them that they are eager to reveal to their hosts.[43] That is why it is important in my research to not only study the welcome and hospitality of the dominant CRC culture but also the response and hospitality of the Iranian members of WCRC. Nouwen writes that hospitality is about creating "a free space where the stranger can enter and become a friend instead of an enemy."[44]

Hyung Jin Kim Sun points out that Mennonite hospitality gives a lot of emphasis to land and space referencing stories of early Anabaptist believers referring to Ps 24 when under threat of being expelled from their land. Ps 24 speaks of the earth as the Lord's and that all space is his gracious provision for both host and guest. God as the ultimate host invites us into his space to appreciate his good gifts. Migrants and the dispossessed are part of God's providence, and radical hospitality is a sign of God's kingdom.[45]

The theme of space is especially important in terms of hospitality towards Muslims according to Matthew Kaemingk. He writes that God made space for humanity on the cross and that the personal experience of receiving hospitality from God must flow over into society. He writes, "Because Christ opened his nail pierced hands to friend and foe alike, his disciples must reflect that posture in all of their interactions with Islam."[46] Andrew Root notes the importance of a focus on divine action in theological reflection. Root calls this "Christopraxis."[47] Kaemingk's theology of hospitality emerges from the Reformed doctrine of justification and God's welcome to humanity. Root also emphasizes justification as a dynamic "that operates between divine action and human action."[48] Ward notes that this focus on divine action is a good

---

43. Nouwen, *Reaching Out*, 66.
44. Nouwen, *Reaching Out*, 71.
45. Kim Sun, "Mennonite Perspective," 301.
46. Kaemingk, *Christian Hospitality*, 186.
47. Ward, *Introducing Practical Theology*, 46.
48. Ward, *Introducing Practical Theology*, 47.

balance to embodied theology that can become very human centric as opposed to Christocentric.[49]

Ward sees a way of combining both embodied theology and divine action into a gospel-focused, lived theology. Such a theology reflects "everyday practices of religious life and embodied in the way that individuals make and remake themselves through sharing in a religious world."[50] Ward writes that the task of practical theology in the church is examining and expressing the dynamics and patterns that exist within lived theology. This can also help to alter patterns that might be unhelpful or problematic.[51] Such lived theology is usually complex and involves many layers.[52] Kaemingk realistically observes that by saying, "Christ's cruciform hospitality does not promise a romantic rainbow-nation of multicultural harmony."[53] Christian hospitality takes sacrifice and may bring both hosts and guests into uncomfortable places.

In a study of Norwegian hospitality, Kaia Rønsdal examines the phenomena of hospitality in spaces of civil society, "where people are, where life is lived, and where they interpret and understand hospitality. I always start in the lived, in the embodied, as humans are situated bodies."[54] The research study for this book is situated in WCRC and the surrounding area of North York in Toronto, Canada. Applying the research theologically to the lived experience of the members as situated bodies is important. Rønsdal details the increasing traffic from Russia into Norway as asylum seekers using the "Arctic Route." She notes, "Hospitality is linked to space, and to practice hospitality is to welcome others into what will become a shared space with the presence of another."[55] Rønsdal notes that while hospitality is difficult to define, it can be observed and explored in the spaces where it is practiced and lived.[56] This makes it a theme that is amenable to practice-led research

---

49. Ward, *Introducing Practical Theology*, 45.
50. Ward, *Introducing Practical Theology*, 65.
51. Ward, *Introducing Practical Theology*, 67.
52. Ward, *Introducing Practical Theology*, 65.
53. Kaemingk, *Christian Hospitality*, 297.
54. Rønsdal, "We Were Invited to Friendships," 21.
55. Rønsdal, "We Were Invited to Friendships," 24.
56. Rønsdal, "We Were Invited to Friendships," 24.

and theological reflection. Rønsdal ties her own Lutheran theology of calling to the practice of hospitality. By linking the two,[57] Rønsdal introduces the concept that hospitality may be resisted and that resistance may have to be overcome through the concept of calling.[58] Where do we see resistance in the call to hospitality and how is that resistance overcome—through preaching and Bible study, or through specific calls to action? As Kaemingk notes, hospitality sometimes requires sacrifice, and this can be uncomfortable for church members. Rønsdal sees one solution in creation theology and identifying humans as co-creators. She quotes Letty M. Russell in pointing out that hospitality is "to assist in God's intention for the mending of creation."[59]

Welcoming Refugees

Today we have many opportunities to welcome refugees into Canadian churches. This has the potential to transform the church today. Oden also sees the possibility of transformation in early Christian writing. She writes, "Early Christians describe with amazement the possibilities of transformation of host, of guest, of community, even of creation when hospitality is shared.[60] Rønsdal challenges the classical idea of a calling to help the other in terms of the binary idea of host and guest. She writes that embodied, enacted hospitality is much more dynamic, bringing those involved into new experiences and interactions.[61] This relates to Kim Sun's Mennonite theology of hospitality. The author notes that space is the Lord's and that God invites us into his space and host. This means that we must make space for the migrant and that we share as host and guest God's good gifts. Such hospitality is a signpost of God's kingdom when it occurs.[62] Having experienced many forced migrations in their history, Mennonites have much to teach the larger church about welcoming the migrant as part of God's providence.

---

57. Rønsdal, "We Were Invited to Friendships," 24.
58. Rønsdal, "We Were Invited to Friendships," 24.
59. Rønsdal, "We Were Invited to Friendships," 30.
60. Oden, ed., *And You Welcomed Me*, 30.
61. Rønsdal, "We Were Invited to Friendships," 33.
62. Kim Sun, "Mennonite Perspective," 298.

Providence should also speak to Reformed believers who give theological weight to God's sovereignty.

Aldiabat, Alsrayheen, Aquino-Russell, Clinton, and Russell studied the lived experiences of Syrian refugees in Canada. The researchers found that their lived experiences affected their health in both positive and negative ways.[63] The authors conclude that more culturally sensitive health care interventions are needed for the proper care of the refugees.[64] Such a lived experience leads to theological reflection through an embodied theology of health care, and the goal of this book is to reflect on such an embodied theology through the lens of lived experience among the members of WCRC. The research on Syrian refugees uses a phenomenological study while my book uses an ethnographic approach, but the goals are similar. The authors note that integrating Syrian refugees into Canadian culture is not without difficulty, and this is also true for Iranian refugees in Canada. The authors found that Syrian refugees needed time to know and understand Canadian culture while Canadians needed time to learn about the background and experience of newcomers. They also found that Syrian refugees needed time and support to find adequate housing, a job for the head of the household, and a family physician.[65] The authors lament that there is not much information about Syrian refugees in Canada, partly because this is a relatively new situation. The researchers note that their findings are parallel to an Ontario Council of Agencies Serving Immigrants (OCASI) Study (2012). The study identified the most prevalent challenges for new immigrants as follows: difficulty securing employment and finding housing; limited English language skills; social isolation; limited participation in social activities; lack of family/social support networks; lack of adequate/required employment skills; and not being accepted by other residents.[66] The study also noted some frustration among parents as children tended to acculturate more quickly and experienced less culture shock than adults did.[67]

---

63. Aldiabat et al., "Lived Experience," 484.
64. Aldiabat et al., "Lived Experience," 484.
65. Aldiabat et al., "Lived Experience," 486.
66. Aldiabat et al., "Lived Experience," 497.
67. Aldiabat et al., "Lived Experience," 498.

Hospitality and Inclusion

Increasing amounts of Burmese refugees were welcomed into Peter Carmen's church. Most of the refugees were from the Chin and Karen people groups of Myanmar and had spent time in refugee camps. Carmen notes two challenges that the congregation faced. One was the human and material needs of the new arrivals. The second was the rapid pace of change for the congregation. When a long-term member was asked about the situation, she responded, "I suppose we are a bit overwhelmed."[68] The church instituted three basic principles or assumptions to guide their integration of the newcomers. First, the newcomers were given full inclusion in life, leadership, and decision making of the church. Second, unity and openness were important to all members, as was existing as one church rather than three. Third, the church was fair in their compassion and service; services were available to all refugees regardless of religious affiliation.[69]

Captari, Shannonhouse, J. N. Hook, Aten, E. Davis, D. Davis, Van Tongeren, and J. R. Hook encourage the development of a theology of refugee care involving cultural humility and a moral foundation of care. The researchers found in their study that politically liberal individuals endorsed less prejudice towards Syrian refugees. However, they found an even more important factor—beyond religious or political views—to be *cultural humility*. Individuals exhibiting cultural humility exhibited positive attitudes towards Syrian refugees. This is because they are open to others and open to difference in general.[70] The authors conclude that rather than trying to change individual's political views, it is better to build on biblical moral foundations of care and fairness that help to create cultural humility.[71] This approach combined with intergroup social contact theory could be a good approach to increasing positive attitudes of welcome among evangelical church members.

The fact that hospitality can take us into uncomfortable places is emphasized in this example of a church stretched to accept many Burmese refugees. Miroslav Volf's reflections on the nature of hospitality in the face of violence and conflict are a central theme in his book

---

68. Carmen, "I Was a Stranger," 13.
69. Carmen, "I Was a Stranger," 13.
70. Captari et al., "Prejudicial and Welcoming Attitudes," 135.
71. Captari et al., "Prejudicial and Welcoming Attitudes," 135.

Exclusion and Embrace. Volf sees the path to inclusion and embrace as beginning in the Trinitarian nature of God, where the members of the Trinity have co-inherence, a mutual interiority or *perichoresis* that exhibits a beautiful reciprocity.[72] This interiority becomes visible in Jesus' making everything he has learned from the Father available to the disciples in order for them to go and bear fruit—and for this reason, Jesus calls them "friends" as the disciples obey the Father's command to love one another (John 15:15). In friendship, we glimpse God's love poured out on his people. Volf expresses Irenaeus's view of God's embrace: "When the Trinity turns towards the world, the Son and the Spirit become, in Irenaeus' beautiful image, the two arms of God by which humanity was made and taken into God's embrace."[73] The fall—and the resulting enmity among people—means that all of humanity experiences exclusion. Volf references this phenomenon of human experience in his writing. Moving from exclusion to inclusion is an important movement for churches that desire to become more multiethnic and incorporate groups such as Persian Canadians.

Welcoming Iranians

While the general focus of this book is on welcome, hospitality, and inclusion, the specific case study involves the welcome of Farsi-speaking Iranians. Roy Oksnevad, in his study of Iranian diaspora congregations, concludes that many Iranian believers suffer from PTSD (Post Traumatic Stress Disorder), "having been spiritually, emotionally and sometimes physically wounded."[74] He observes that "the hope for a normal life was crushed under oppressive Islamic regimes" and that "despair has given birth to high alcoholism, drug use, and suicide rates" in Iran.[75] This trauma has also led to a lot of suspicion, fear, and a survival mentality among believers that drives "survival of the fittest" behaviour. This negativity affects communication in the church. Oksnevad found in interviews that informants were suspicious, looking for ulterior motives. This means that Iranians are often afraid to share

72. Volf, *Exclusion and Embrace*, 128.
73. Volf, *Exclusion and Embrace*, 128.
74. Oksnevad, *Burden of Baggage*, 155.
75. Oksnevad, *Burden of Baggage*, 155.

information and resources. For these reasons, it is important to be aware of trauma in the WCRC context among Iranian members. Could hospitality in this context involve making space for trauma healing and emotional and spiritual health?

It is important to recognize that a theology of trauma healing is an important part of welcoming Persians. Resmaa Menakem argues in his book *My Grandmothers Hands* that humans carry trauma in their bodies. White bodies carry trauma from past wars and conflicts and since 9/11 and subsequent wars in the Middle East. They also carry trauma from news reports of terrorist attacks, which affect how white bodies react to brown or Middle Eastern bodies.[76] Although Menakem is mainly talking about the highly racialized situation in the US, his thinking can be applied to Christian Reformed Church members opening their arms in embrace of Middle Eastern people from Iran. A theology of trauma healing considers how people react in their bodies in fight and flight mode in ways that they might not be conscious. At the same time, many Iranian immigrants to Canada carry trauma from their life in Iran and their time journeying to Canada through refugee camps in places like Turkey. Though Persians have a proud history, they are very aware of the difficult political situation in Iran since the Islamic revolution in 1979. This is especially true for Christian believers coming out of secret house churches in Iran. As a case in point, a friend of mine who is an Iranian believer gave his testimony at a church event. However, in the process of recounting his story, this individual was re-traumatized and decided to stop sharing his testimony publicly. I learned that one must be very careful in asking for testimonies from refugees as they have so often experienced trauma in their refugee journey. The American Bible Society runs the Trauma Healing Institute (traumahealinginstitute.org) that helps traumatized populations find healing.

Connected to this question of trauma is the shame and honour worldview that is a part of Iranian culture. People from Middle Eastern cultures exhibit a shame–honour paradigm in terms of their relationships and attitudes towards forgiveness and sanctification. Werner Mischke writes in his book *The Global Gospel* about honour-shame issues: "I've become convicted that the cultural dynamic of *honor and*

76. Menakem, *My Grandmother's Hands*, 54–55.

shame—in understanding, communicating, and living out the gospel of Christ—is an important strategic issue for world missions."[77] Therefore, it is important to show that Jesus does not only forgive sins by means of his penal substitutionary atonement but also heals shame and restores honour, through his death on the cross. Shame is often associated with being unclean or impure in such societies, but in many of Jesus' healing miracles, there is not only physical healing but also healing from shame and impurity. One example comes from Mark 5:25–34 where a woman seeks healing from physical bleeding that makes her ritually unclean. Jesus not only heals her physically but also restores her honour in her community and heals her shame. Nabeel Jabbour notes that biblical readers in the Western world can have blind spots, and readers from the Middle East and other parts of the world can help them see the Bible in newer ways, particularly in terms of shame–honour and fear–power paradigms.[78] Oksnevad found that the Iranian church is growing out of little collective memory of the church.[79] This means that there is not a long history of discipleship and leadership development. Oksnevad notes that there is a need to move away from a shame-based way of doing ministry into a more God-directed service model, which requires a major shift in worldview. Creating healthy boundaries, developing transparency and an ability to be vulnerable are important, though a cross-cultural challenge for many Iranian believers.[80]

Recognition and Friendship

Another fundamental aspect of hospitality and inclusion is recognition. To see the other in this biblical sense is to recognize them. About the power of recognition, Christine Pohl writes, "recognition involves respecting the dignity and worth of every person and valuing their contributions, to the larger community."[81] Recognition begins with recognizing Jesus in the stranger as outlined in Matt 25. Recognizing Jesus in the stranger gives them dignity and worth and a warm welcome. The

---

77. Mischke, *Global Gospel*, 25.
78. Jabbour, *Crescent through the Eyes of the Cross*, 152.
79. Oksnevad, *Burden of Baggage*, 155.
80. Oksnevad, *Burden of Baggage*, 156.
81. Pohl, *Making Room*, 61.

other part of recognition is the "two-way street" role of hospitality. The host is blessed by the guest, the guest by the host, and together the realization that both are helping each other in mutuality.[82] Recognition is all about the affirmation of human personhood. Pohl says, "simple acts of respect and appreciation, presence and friendship are indispensable parts of the affirmation of human personhood."[83] Recognition is an important part of welcoming the other and this is particularly true for Christian Reformed churches welcoming Persian seekers and new believers. Recognition leads to possibilities for friendship.

Pohl concludes her chapter on recognition by referring to the Salvation Army and their ability to help the friendless of the world find friends. She refers to true hospitality as involving friendship that "brings to the other what no law or revolution can do: understanding and acceptance."[84] Brother John of Taizé sees friendship as a way of coming to know better the message of Christ. Jesus has made all believers his friends (John 15:15), which then makes friendship possible among groups of people who come from different cultures, ethnic backgrounds, and geographical locations. Believers are tied together in Christ and are part of the body of Christ (1 Cor 12). This is not just an intellectual assent to become friends with others, particularly strangers, but a way of life that is "summed up in the command to love one another."[85] Friendship with God is possible through Christ. We are not enemies of God but friends. This makes it possible to be friends with others and to take on an attitude of friendliness. It is now possible to make friends with all, even with those whom we have little in common with and might even consider an enemy.[86] This kind of friendship leads to a diverse global church manifested in local congregations. This allows for the integration of Persians and Persian fellowships into existing Christian Reformed congregations. It also allows for conversation with Iranian immigrants who are Muslims and who are interested in dialogue with Christians. Friendships can cross physical and religious

82. Pohl, *Making Room*, 72.
83. Pohl, *Making Room*, 84.
84. Pohl, *Making Room*, 84.
85. Brother John of Taizé, *Friends in Christ*, 89.
86. Brother John of Taizé, *Friends in Christ*, 129.

boundaries when lived out as an ethic of loving the neighbour. Mona Siddiqui writes in her book *Hospitality and Islam*, "in our globalized world where different cultures, races and religions are coming together, even colliding in private and public spaces, friendship assumes a new and more potent significance."[87] Friendship involves risks, which speaks to the fear that many hold of the other, but it also has benefits. Siddiqui notes that, "if a friendship unsettles us, it ultimately opens us to thinking about who we are as people and how and in whom we seek happiness and wisdom."[88]

Inclusion

Once a regular practice of welcoming is established, the next step is enfolding and discipling new believers well—so many of the Persian community are new believers from an Islamic background. Sandra Van Opstal writes in the context of worship leadership that it is not enough just to welcome some people of different ethnicities and cultures onto the worship team. This can result in mere tokenism. It is important to allow them to lead from their own cultural background. This involves listening and understanding, which Van Opstal refers to as solidarity with the other, and then in time, really needing the other, which Van Opstal calls mutuality.[89] In the case of congregations welcoming Persian believers, it may be too early to research how this process of discipleship and leadership development is progressing, but it is important to understand this progression in order to strive towards the development of fully formed and spiritually healthy believers. Mark Deymaz points to the importance of worship for the full inclusion of newcomers. He writes, "to build a healthy multi-ethnic church, then, it is in worship that leaders must begin to promote a spirit of inclusion."[90] This would point to the importance of bringing the Farsi language into worship where possible, rather than expecting everyone to switch to English.[91]

---

87. Siddiqui, *Hospitality and Islam*, 236.
88. Siddiqui, *Hospitality and Islam*, 239.
89. Van Opstal, *Next Worship*, 75.
90. Deymaz, *Building a Healthy Multi-Ethnic Church*, 109.

91. It should be noted, however, that English language use does have some advantages. It benefits newcomers to Canada by helping them learn one of the

Hospitality and Inclusion

There are different approaches to the discipleship of believers from a Muslim background as Don Little outlines in his book *Effective Discipling in Muslim Communities*. Little examines patterns of discipleship in Luke–Acts and concludes that discipleship is about setting aside old allegiances and entering life in the community of the Spirit.[92] One of the challenges for new believers from a Muslim background is the pressure exerted on these new converts by their family and friends to revert to the Islamic faith. Little believes that for this reason it is important that the new believer is "welcomed into vital, Spirit-filled groups of believers, which are experiencing the realities of the new covenant community together."[93] New believers from a Muslim background flourish when they experience the power of the Holy Spirit flowing through a community of mutual love and care. This is also important for Oksnevad, according to his study of Iranian fellowships, because new believers from a Muslim background tend towards legalism and chronic shame. It is only through the active work of the Holy Spirit that believers can be healed of their shame and learn that life in the Spirit is their new goal. Further, in order to grow in faith, they need to put off the old self (leaving their Islamic faith behind) and put on the new self in Christ (Eph 4:22–24; Col 3:9–10). They also need to experience a renewing of their mind (Rom 12:1–2). To hold on to old Islamic beliefs can only be confusing and detrimental to their new faith journey. That is why putting off and on and renewal of the mind are important concepts for the new believer from an Islamic background.[94]

In the book *Miraculous Movements*, Jerry Trousdale lists evidence of transformation in new believers from an Islamic background who have experienced the gospel including healing in families, a spirit of freedom, a spirit of love, diminished violence, less addiction, redemption and hope, evidence of divine favour, grace in persecution, freedom from demonic oppression, and the power of individual prayer.[95]

---

official languages of Canada and thus become eligible for employment and social advancement.

92. Little, *Effective Discipling*, 71.
93. Little, *Effective Discipling*, 72.
94. Oksnevad, *Burden of Baggage*, 152.
95. Trousdale, *Miraculous Movements*, 124–6.

Little observes that one of the biggest obstacles to growth in faith for Muslim-background believers is pressure from family and community, including hostility, ongoing control, and rejection from their Muslim community.[96] For this reason, church communities must fill in the gap of lost family. Mentors are especially important to help new converts weather these relational and emotional challenges.

Langmead observes that "Christian churches are a sign of God's welcome when they are hospitable multicultural faith communities."[97] Langmead defines multicultural ministry as "creating a safe and welcoming space for those who are different from each other, especially those who are strangers to the dominant culture."[98] A hospitable multicultural church is "intentional in its welcome, embracing difference as a gift." Finally, "it makes space for people's unique stories" and works to ensure diversity in all aspects of the life of the church. It is more event oriented than program oriented.[99]

In the face of change, churches need to manage anxiety. According to Chris Pullenayegem, congregations often experience two types of anxiety: one type is called "survival anxiety," and the other "learning anxiety."[100] While survival anxiety is about remaining the same, learning anxiety is associated with change.[101] For Pullenayegem, it is important for churches to manage these anxieties so that survival anxiety is greater than learning anxiety.[102] This will motivate people to change. Such change is necessary for hospitality to happen and for hosts to be able to become vulnerable enough to become guests.

For a theological perspective on encouraging diversity in a congregational context, we turn to Volf, who writes of the importance of the Pentecost passage in Acts 2:1–13 as central to the understanding of our unity in Christ exhibiting diversity and who argues that diversity in the church is an outgrowth of God's reconciling work in the

---

96. Little, *Effective Discipling*, 179.
97. Langmead, "Refugees as Guests and Hosts," 42.
98. Langmead, "Refugees as Guests and Hosts," 42.
99. Langmead, "Refugees as Guests and Hosts," 42.
100. Pullenayegem, "Surviving or Thriving?" 182.
101. Pullenayegem, "Surviving or Thriving?" 182.
102. Pullenayegem, "Surviving or Thriving?" 182.

world through his Spirit. According to Volf in *Exclusion and Embrace*, Pentecost is the redemption of Babel in the Old Testament when the people were scattered and their language mixed up. It is through the Holy Spirit that God celebrates unity in diversity.[103] God does not return to a pre-Babel scenario where people all begin to speak one language so that they understand each other. Instead, the Holy Spirit gives the disciples the ability to speak in many different languages, and the diverse crowd there from different parts of the Roman Empire could understand them. God values diversity. This is important in a setting where different cultures and languages are mixing. It points to seeing diversity as a beautiful part of God's creation and new creation and not a problem to solve through mono-cultural homogeneity. It points to the importance of language and honouring the heart languages of the other. Yong writes that as the church bears witness to Jesus Christ in a post-Christendom and post-modern world, her praxis needs to take many forms, "and this multiplicity of forms is manifest in the diversity of tongues and gifts of the Spirit."[104]

Evergreen Church is a good example of a multi-cultural church exhibiting hospitality in a multicultural context. Kathleen Garces-Foley writes about this Asian American church in Southern California that has become increasingly multicultural and the church's ongoing opportunities and challenges that have come with that change. Garces-Foley notes three challenging areas for people: communication, food, and marriage. This is because these three aspects of life are valued within specific cultures, and losing them is difficult, particularly for the first generation of immigrant members.[105] For this reason, I designed the project to listen to both long-term members of WCRC as well as the newer members from Iran.

Biblically speaking, the multicultural church today looks in eschatological hope towards the vision of John of Patmos described in Rev 5:9. God's throne is surrounded by believers who have been purchased by the blood of Christ for salvation, and these believers are from different tribes, languages, peoples, and nations. United together

---

103. Volf, *Exclusion and Embrace*, 228.
104. Yong, *Hospitality and the Other*, 64.
105. Garces-Foley, *Crossing the Ethnic Divide*, 104.

they all give praise and glory to the Lamb Jesus Christ in their diverse languages. Robert Mounce, in his commentary on Revelation, identifies those purchased by the blood of Christ coming from every tribe, language, people, and nation as a way for the Seer to stress the universal nature of the church as compared to the exclusivist nature of Judaism. Mounce sees this as a rhetorical device to identify the church as ecumenical, with no national, political, cultural, or racial boundaries.[106] This is an important vision for the church today in the "already and not yet" times of this present day. As the church welcomes the other who is from a different tribe, language, people, and nation, we begin to live out this vision more fully until Christ returns and this vision comes to full fruition.

A New Perspective

This welcome by the church necessitates a shift from a cultural dynamic of Christendom and power to a more marginalized position in Canadian society. Alan Roxburgh sees this as a shift from a focus on the Great Commission (Matt 28) to the sending out of the seventy-two disciples in Luke 10. The shift is from an old colonial mindset of bringing a Western perspective for the gospel in missional work to a more respectful approach of humility and mutual understanding. The disciples go out in need, taking neither a bag nor sandals, and become dependent on the hosts that they encounter in the form of persons of peace. This is a paradigm shift and part of giving the early believers in Luke's time a new language house for missions.[107] Roxburgh observes that "the Spirit is pushing apart the settled, managed and controlled ecclesiologies that came out of specific period of European history."[108]

Mark Branson and Alan Roxburgh discuss the importance of *habitus* and practice for church leaders experiencing change and disruption.[109] Mark Branson and Juan Martinez discuss sociocultural structures and ethnicity in churches embracing intercultural life.[110]

---

106. Mounce, *Book of Revelation*, 136.
107. Roxburgh, *Missional*, 66.
108. Roxburgh, *Missional*, 114.
109. Branson and Roxburgh, *Leadership*, 169.
110. Branson and Martinez, *Churches*, 89.

Hospitality and Inclusion

Nancy Ammerman writes on culture and identity in the context of congregations. Her perspective from a congregational studies perspective is helpful. She notes that new members bring changes to the culture of a congregation; she writes, "they bring in new expectations, new experiences and new connections to other parts of the community."[111] Specific to Iranian culture, Werner Mischke writes on the implications of the gospel with shame-and-honour societies. Shame-and-honour issues are present in Iranian communities, and so insights into Christ's reversal of shame in his journey through humiliation and exaltation is helpful.[112] God as a patron of grace and blessing is a helpful theological insight for discussing the cultural challenge of patron and client dynamics in Iranian communities.[113]

Peter von Kaehne reflects on his experience of attending an Iranian church in Glasgow, Scotland. He observes that there is a vibrant prayer ministry with individuals showing a "stunning trust" in the power of prayer.[114] Their policy towards baptism is to baptize all who request it and not to question motives, while supporting asylum applications and giving testimony in court. They do not directly address Islam, finding that many Iranians are not directly tied to Islam, but they do address patterns of thought such as works versus grace and leadership models.[115] From time to time, they have experienced conflict, mainly around arrogance, pride, and hidden or uncontrolled anger. Reconciliation, usually preceded by a humble and honest apology tends to be lasting.[116]

Sacramental Hospitality

Von Kaehne's observation on baptism points to an important source of hospitality in the church, the sacraments. Eucharistic hospitality is an important aspect of welcome as is baptism as initiation, both into the Christian faith and into membership in the church. Vander Zee points

111. Ammerman, "Cultural and Identity," 90.
112. Mischke, *Global Gospel*, 274.
113. Mischke, *Global Gospel*, 254.
114. von Kaehne, "Iranian Diaspora Ministry," 445.
115. von Kaehne, "Iranian Diaspora Ministry," 445.
116. von Kaehne, "Iranian Diaspora Ministry," 445–46.

out that in the Reformed tradition, the central act of baptism belongs to God.[117] This is an important principle because it means that God is the host when people come to be baptized and God is welcoming them into his church. In the sacrament of baptism, the physical has an important place as the water is a sign of union with Christ that is felt and experienced, so it is embodied hospitality.[118] Baptism is into the one body of Christ, so it also brings unity.[119]

Claudio Carvalhaes notes that John Calvin wanted to celebrate the Eucharist every Sunday, but the city council of Geneva overruled him. For Calvin, the Lord's Supper was a source of "both spiritual nourishment and fraternal love."[120] This was one of the reasons Calvin believed in frequent participation in the Lord's Supper. Carvalhaes notes that, in Calvin's conception of the Lord's Supper, in the real spiritual presence of Jesus, the power was taken away from the institutional church and given to the Holy Spirit and the work of faith in the heart of the believer.[121] This shift in locus of power is important once again in emphasizing that God is the host and all who participate in the church are guests, which points to the mutuality of all believers in the church. All—long-term members, newcomers, rich, and poor—are guests at the table of the Lord. God is not contained in the elements or the institution but is free to move. In the Lord's Supper, bread and wine (or juice) are consumed, but real nourishment is spiritual.[122] This is another example then of embodied hospitality. Our bodies become "a privileged locus of God's revelation,"[123] according to Carvalhaes. Chester points out that regular participation in the Lord's Supper transforms the identity of the believer because it enrolls the believer in the story of God and "connects past and present through Spirit-empowered remembrance."[124]

---

117. Vander Zee, *Christ, Baptism and the Lord's Supper*, 102.
118. Vander Zee, *Christ, Baptism and the Lord's Supper*, 106.
119. Vander Zee, *Christ, Baptism and the Lord's Supper*, 110.
120. Carvalhaes, *Eucharist and Globalization*, 109.
121. Carvalhaes, *Eucharist and Globalization*, 90.
122. Carvalhaes, *Eucharist and Globalization*, 106.
123. Carvalhaes, *Eucharist and Globalization*, 116.
124. Chester, *Truth We Can Touch*, 112.

THEORETICAL FOUNDATIONS

I intend to explore Social Contact theory and Social Identity theory as a factor in in-group and out-group interaction. According to the theory, such contact reduces prejudice, whether it is extended, vicarious or direct. As there is a long tradition of theological thought around hospitality in the church, social contact theory also postulates that contact between groups and increased familiarity will lead to reduced prejudice and more openness to the other. Social contact theory is an appropriate social conversation partner for our theological reflection on the embodied theology reflected in the practices, rituals, and culture of hospitality among the members of WCRC.

Social Contact Theory

Gordon Allport was the creator of the cognitive theory of social contact. In his book *The Nature of Prejudice*, he writes that while we are "learning to control physical suffering and premature death . . . by contrast we appear to be living in the Stone Age as far as our handling of human relationships is concerned."[125] His concern with prejudice among groups and the effect of cognitive strategies such as categorization led him to develop cognitive social contact theory. According to this theory, humans seek to simplify their relationships with out-groups by forming generalizations, concepts, and categories that are both rational and irrational. A stereotype is an "exaggerated belief associated with a category."[126] Allport concluded that social contact can reduce prejudice when it involves groups that are of equal status and are in the process of pursuing common goals.[127] Such common goals also lead to a new combined identity.

Michelle Ortiz and Jake Harwood looked at the effects of social cognitive theory on intergroup attitudes. Intergroup contact is "an effective approach for the reduction of prejudice, negative stereotyping and discrimination."[128] They note that negative emotions such as

---

125. Allport, *Nature of Prejudice*, ix.
126. Allport, *Nature of Prejudice*, 187.
127. Allport, *Nature of Prejudice*, 267.
128. Ortiz and Harwood, "Social Cognitive Theory," 615.

anxiety are high in intergroup contact. Anxious people rely more on stereotypes. But anxiety is reduced by establishing clear expectations for behaviour.[129] Social cognitive theory predicts that humans can learn from observation and "can internalize cognitive, affective and behavioral responses to situations they do not experience directly."[130] Individuals can learn positive behaviours and attitudes through intergroup contact. The authors were able to show an association between positive intergroup contact and positive intergroup attitudes in a mediated approach.[131] It was noted that "knowledge of an intergroup friendship involving an in-group member is enough to lead to positive attitude change."[132] While this study was mainly involving the effects of media, it is reasonable to assume these kinds of social cognitive effects could also be occurring in the WCRC context of intergroup contact. Clearly, reducing anxiety and improving attitudes in intergroup contact are desirable goals for congregations like WCRC that are experiencing cross-cultural change.

There are limits, however, to the effect of social contact. It is important to note that optimal conditions are needed for social contact to reduce prejudice. These conditions are equal status, cooperation to achieve superordinate goals, and support from institutions and norms.[133] After six decades of research, Vezzali and Stathi conclude that there is clear evidence that social contact reduces prejudice. They also note that while this theory is not a panacea, it is a useful tool in improving intergroup relations.[134] In studying long-term contact, Vezzali and Stathi observe, "individuals may learn positive responses towards the out-group by observing the in-group peers interacting with out-group members."[135] One possible reason for this is that observing such interactions causes vicarious cognitive dissonance that leads to attitude

129. Ortiz and Harwood, "Social Cognitive Theory," 616.
130. Ortiz and Harwood, "Social Cognitive Theory," 617.
131. Ortiz and Harwood, "Social Cognitive Theory," 628.
132. Ortiz and Harwood, "Social Cognitive Theory," 628.
133. Vezzali and Stathi, "The Present and the Future of the Contact Hypothesis," 2.
134. Vezzali and Stathi, "The Present and the Future of the Contact Hypothesis," 2.
135. Vezzali and Stathi, "Extended Intergroup Contact Hypothesis," 116.

change.[136] Additional reasons are the reduction in anxiety that prevents positive intergroup responses as well as familiarity with in-group and out-group norms.[137]

Such contact theories could be at work in the WCRC community. As the authors note, it is less threatening to have indirect contact with an out-group member. It is also true that observing an in-group member interacting positively with the out-group can have beneficial effects. These kinds of extended and vicarious intergroup contact effects could reduce prejudice and promote positive attitudes among in-group participants towards out-group members in the WCRC congregation. As anxiety and attitudes are aligned, resulting from cognitive dissonance in observing positive intergroup relationships and norms, it is possible that relations will improve in such a church community context.

Marianne Carlson et al. examine the effects of religious belief and personality on prejudice towards Syrian refugees in the US.[138] They find that religious belief does influence prejudice depending on whether such beliefs are internalized or externalized. Individuals with higher levels of internalization have less prejudice, unless such prejudice is sanctioned by the religious group. Individuals who have more extrinsic beliefs and tend to compartmentalize their religious beliefs tend to be more prejudiced.[139] The researchers predict that participants most open to refugees and newcomers would be those categorized as having a quest orientation—one that reflects openness to faith and is "often being shaped through complex questions, curiosities and doubts."[140] They also observe that personality accounts for about 15 percent of the attitudes of the informants, with those who exhibit the personality trait of agreeableness being the most open to newcomers and expressing the least prejudice.[141] They also see a correlation with those who demonstrate a quest religious orientation—those who have an internalized religious profile have less correlation but do exhibit more

---

136. Vezzali and Stathi, "Extended Intergroup Contact Hypothesis," 116.
137. Vezzali and Stathi, "Extended Intergroup Contact Hypothesis," 117.
138. Carlson et al., "We Welcome Refugees?"
139. Carlson et al., "We Welcome Refugees?" 96.
140. Carlson et al., "We Welcome Refugees?" 96.
141. Carlson et al., "We Welcome Refugees?" 102.

prejudice.¹⁴² While considering religious orientation and personality types is beyond the scope of this book, it is good to be aware of these variables in intergroup contact. It shows that while intergroup contact can have positive effects, there are other factors such as individual personalities that will affect the cohesion of in-groups and out-groups. Jeffery Dixon and Michael Rosenbaum identify a limitation to contact theory that "more prejudiced individuals may avoid contact with minorities limiting its effect."[143] However, other types of contact such as vicarious or extended contact may still reach such individuals through friends or family in the in-group.

Captari, Shannonhouse, J. N. Hook, Aten, E. Davis, D. Davis, Van Tongeren, and J. R. Hook observe that in encouraging engagement with refugees among evangelical church members, intergroup contact theory "would suggest the importance of advocacy that facilitates positive direct contact between groups."[144] They further note that such contact "should enable genuine closeness and meaningful relationships across group boundaries, and be based on cooperation between members of different cultural groups in such a way that there is mutual dependence."[145] They also suggest working with non-profit agencies and organizations that serve refugees to build this intergroup contact in a collaborative long term way.[146]

Social Identity Theory

Social identity theory was developed by Henri Tajfel, a holocaust survivor who explored inter-group dynamics and identity in the context of post-World War II Europe. Tajfel was involved in rehabilitating victims of war—both children and adults—which led him to an interest in social psychology.[147] Tajfel defines social identity as "that part of an individual's self-concept which derives from his knowledge of his membership in a social group (or groups) together with the value

---

142. Carlson et al., "We Welcome Refugees?" 102.
143. Dixon and Rosenbaum, "Nice to Know You?" 261.
144. Captari et al., "Prejudicial and Welcoming Attitudes," 135.
145. Captari et al., "Prejudicial and Welcoming Attitudes," 135.
146. Captari et al., "Prejudicial and Welcoming Attitudes," 135.
147. Tajfel, *Human Groups and Social Categories*, 1–2.

or emotional significance attached to that membership."[148] One of the consequences of this theory is that individuals will remain members of groups or join new groups if these groups in some way contribute to positive aspects of the individual's social identity.[149] Related to social identity is social categorization. In this case, a group becomes a group "because other groups are present in the environment."[150] One aspect of this that we can study is the identity transformation that occurs when Iranians become Christians and experience initiation into the Christian faith and church through baptism. How does such a transformation contribute to positive aspects of the individual's social identity?

Dominic Abrams and Michael Hogg define social identity as "the individual's knowledge that he/she belongs to certain social groups together with some emotional and value significance to him/her of the group membership."[151] They also describe it as "self-conception as a group member" which plays a central role in the process of categorization which partitions the world into comprehensible units."[152] Further, the theory posits that "one's social identity is also clarified through social comparison, but generally the comparison between in-groups and out-groups."[153] If the in-group is perceived as both different and better than the out-group, "one's social identity is enhanced."[154]

Social identity theory is necessary for evaluating intergroup contact because social identity leads to categorization as "a key feature of human social cognition."[155] Perry Hinton gives the example of an observer waiting at a bus stop looking for a person (actor) to ask why the bus is late. Since they are all strangers, they fall into different categories—young mothers, elderly, professionals, or foreign looking. The observer may not be a member of any of these groups, but if she is, for example, a young mother, then she would form an in-group with

---

148. Tajfel, *Human Groups and Social Categories*, 255.
149. Tajfel, *Human Groups and Social Categories*, 256.
150. Tajfel, *Human Groups and Social Categories*, 258.
151. Abrams and Hogg, "Introduction to the Social Identity Approach," 2.
152. Abrams and Hogg, "Introduction to the Social Identity Approach," 2.
153. Abrams and Hogg, "Introduction to the Social Identity Approach," 3.
154. Abrams and Hogg, "Introduction to the Social Identity Approach," 3.
155. Hinton, *Perception of People*, 54.

the young mother and the others would form an out-group. This is both a perception and an allocation of in- and out-groups.[156] Fathali Moghaddam ties intergroup theory to identity: "Increased intergroup contact is leading to a greater focus on identity, as individuals from different groups present themselves to one another and explain 'the kinds of persons they are.'"[157]

In line with social identity, people tend to categorize themselves on different levels from the concrete to the abstract, depending on the context. For example, in some situations, a person might categorize him- or herself according to individual interests or hobbies, and in other situations, according to a group activity such as a fan club.[158] The choice of category often depends on how salient the category is—for example, a woman may choose the category of female in a room of men. This theory shows the importance of social identity based on social categorization on personal perception. One can predict that social identity would need to shift to allow in-group and out-group interaction across social categories in the WCRC community.

Michael Hogg surveys the origins of social identity theory and notes that since the 1970s there has been an increased focus on the categorization process in in-group identity formation leading to the development of self-categorization theory of the "social identity theory of the group."[159] One tension in social identity theory, according to Moghaddam, is a "tension between personal identity and social identity of individuals who emphasize their personal characteristics and stand outside of groups as opposed to those who want to 'belong' and be accepted as group members."[160] It is this tension between being accepted and standing outside that leads to self-categorization. Optimal distinctiveness theory is similar because "only it focuses more directly on the cognitive strategies that can be used to balance 'standing outside of' and 'belonging to' groups."[161] This theory explains the comparisons that

---

156. Hinton, *Perception of People*, 55.
157. Moghaddam, *Multiculturalism and Intergroup Relations*, 91.
158. Hinton, *Perception of People*, 57.
159. Hogg, "Social Identity Theory," 113.
160. Moghaddam, *Multiculturalism and Intergroup Relations*, 100.
161. Moghaddam, *Multiculturalism and Intergroup Relations*, 101.

people make between the in-group and the out-group as a cognitive strategy for meeting the need for both inclusion and distinctiveness.[162] This theory provides balance between identification with an in-group and differentiation between in-groups and out-groups.[163] Combining intergroup research with social identity around the themes of inclusion and exclusion, Moghaddam notes, through re-categorization of the social world, "group members come to perceive themselves as belonging to subgroups encompassed by a superordinate group identity."[164] If the salience of a common in-group identity increases, "a superordinate identity will come to dominate social relations without individuals abandoning their less inclusive group memberships (such as those based on ethnicity)."[165] One could hypothesize that forming a superordinate identity as Christian Reformed members of WCRC could lead to more inclusion and less intergroup conflict.

SUMMARY

This chapter has built a foundation for integrating social theory of welcome with biblical and theological foundations of welcoming the other in order to understand and evaluate the experience of welcome at WCRC. The challenge is to understand the embodied theology of the congregation as two very different groups in contact. The way in which they understand each other and how that understanding has changed over time will be explored. The practices and rituals of welcome for both host and guest and the mutuality of the experience of hospitality must be evaluated within a long tradition of hospitality that emphasizes the stranger as the image of God and the face of Christ. This includes the Persian stranger in the Canadian context. Specific issues such as trauma, honour and shame issues, and other cultural phenomena, affect the welcome experience of the Persian guest as well as the host. How is the congregation at WCRC experiencing these challenges? How does a changing congregation affect the long-term members? How are both groups blessed together in their superordinate identity as members of

---

162. Moghaddam, *Multiculturalism and Intergroup Relations*, 101.
163. Moghaddam, *Multiculturalism and Intergroup Relations*, 101.
164. Moghaddam, *Multiculturalism and Intergroup Relations*, 102.
165. Moghaddam, *Multiculturalism and Intergroup Relations*, 102.

WCRC as they together move from being us versus them to a mutuality that strengthens the church?

Volf sees exclusion occurring because identity "arises out of the complex history of 'differentiation' in which both the self and the other take part by negotiating their identities in interaction with one another."[166] Exclusion, according to Volf, is the reconfiguring of creation that breaks our interdependence and creative encounter with the other. This is a direct result of sin that "puts asunder what God has joined."[167] How do intergroup contact and social identity in the context of hospitality help to "reconfigure creation" and how is God at work in such situations? How does our theology of welcoming the other help a congregation in the worship and preaching and the regular practice of the sacraments? How does social contact and biblical friendship contribute to the reduction of anxiety and prejudice and the building of bonds of fellowship? These are areas to explore and reflect on in this ethnographic study.

---

166. Volf, *Exclusion and Embrace*, 66.
167. Volf, *Exclusion and Embrace*, 66.

Chapter 3

Research Methodology

THIS PROJECT USES A qualitative ethnographic research method. This method is well suited to the specific congregational context of WCRC. In this chapter, I explain the method, including how the participants were recruited and interviewed and how the data were analyzed including participant inputs and meanings. I also employ participant observation over the two-and-one-half months of the study period.

The research problem is the challenge of welcoming the other who is a stranger and from a very different cultural and ethnic background. In the case study of WCRC, the focus is the welcome of Iranians, a group that is very different culturally from the Dutch Canadian host community. It is worth noting that there are three families from the Philippines and one with Korean roots in the congregation, but the original community mainly arises from post-World War II immigration from the Netherlands. The research puzzle behind this question is both developmental and mechanical.[1] The purpose of this research study is to understand the development and ongoing practices, rituals, and attitudes around a culture of welcome, hospitality, and inclusion of the newer Farsi speaking members of the church. As the research question relates directly to the culture in the church and the embodied theology of hospitality, a qualitative research method is used. Qualitative research methodology can be effective for understanding the experience of informants from both the host culture and the guest culture.

1. Moschella, *Ethnography as a Pastoral Practice*, 57.

I observed two regular weekly gatherings to gain more information about the congregation and their weekly practices and rituals. The two gatherings were the Sunday morning service and the Thursday evening Farsi Fellowship meeting. Other weekly events continued in the church but were curtailed due to COVID-19 restrictions. Regular events in the church included an ESL (English as a Second Language) Bible study, a hymn singing, and two regular Bible studies. I did not attend these events but focused on the two larger meetings. I also interviewed nine informants.

A further focus of this study is to understand the lived behaviour of both the host and the guest communities and the mutual dynamic of giving and receiving within the context of a changing congregation. I employ Spradley's ethnographic methodology because it gives the researcher a specific protocol coding method called the "developmental sequence." This method is a pre-established and standardized system of coding qualitative data. Saldana, in outlining different coding systems, notes, "protocols provide much of the preparatory work for the new investigator."[2] Saldana cautions the researcher to "assess a protocol critically and, if necessary, adapt the guidelines to suit your own research contexts."[3] Depending on the transferability and trustworthiness of the protocol, some protocols "may also contribute to the reliability and validity (i.e. credibility) of the researcher's new study."[4] This method also helps the researcher to hear the *voice* of the informants and to apply meaning into the use of their native terms as keys to understanding their worldview rather than apply meaning to them from outside. The idea is to increase the voice of the congregants and reduce the voice of the researcher.

Qualitative methodology is a way of understanding the world through the production of formal statements and conceptual frameworks. These frameworks provide new ways of understanding the world and specifically the culture and practices involved in welcome and inclusion of Persian newcomers at WCRC.[5] Qualitative research is

2. Saldana, *Coding Manual*, 232.
3. Saldana, *Coding Manual*, 232.
4. Saldana, *Coding Manual*, 230.
5. Swinton and Mowat, *Practical Theology*, 30.

helpful for practical-theological research because it "feeds into practice and enables people to develop in-depth understanding of those whom they encounter and seek to understand."[6] Qualitative research also leads to understanding of meaning of complex phenomena and reflexive knowing on the part of the researcher.[7] An important epistemological assumption in such research is constructivism. This perspective assumes that "truth and knowledge and the ways that it is perceived by human beings and communities is, to a greater or lesser extent, constructed by individuals and communities."[8] Swinton and Mowat note, from a Christian perspective, that a form of mediated or critical realism is more appropriate because such constructions are always open to challenge.[9] Qualitative research diverges from the natural sciences in that it is not for objective explanation but rather for a deeper understanding of situations. It thus has an interpretative dimension in reflecting critically on the nature of situations.[10] In ethnographic research, the researcher generates knowledge through first-hand experience.[11]

Webb examines the question of sample size in qualitative research and notes a progression in qualitative research from a desire for larger sample size (which replicates quantitative methodology) to a goal of saturation. That means that a smaller sample size of eight to twelve informants is sufficient if there are multiple interviews per person and thus more data are collected. The idea of saturation is more important. Saturation occurs "when you cease getting new information and redundancy becomes apparent."[12] For this reason, Spradley's ethnographic method is helpful for reaching saturation. Spradley's developmental sequence involves a series of three interviews per informant allowing for more in-depth understanding and analysis of the situation.

---

6. Swinton and Mowat, *Practical Theology*, 32.
7. Swinton and Mowat, *Practical Theology*, 33.
8. Swinton and Mowat, *Practical Theology*, 34.
9. Swinton and Mowat, *Practical Theology*, 36.
10. Swinton and Mowat, *Practical Theology*, 36.
11. Mason, *Qualitative Researching*, 8.
12. Webb, *So You Want to Do a Qualitative Dissertation?* 102.

ETHNOGRAPHY AS A RESEARCH METHODOLOGY

Ethnography is a good methodology for studying the attitudes, practices, rituals, and culture of welcome and hospitality at WCRC. Spradley observes that ethnography is less about collecting "data" about people and more about seeking to learn from people "to be taught by them."[13] Its essential core is a concern "with the meaning of actions and events to the people we seek to understand."[14] In terms of observing a culture of welcome in the congregational context studied, Spradley defines culture as "behavior patterns associated with particular groups of people, that is to 'customs,' or to a people's 'way of life.'"[15] Ethnography has potential as a methodology for understanding the life of a congregation. Lynda Mannik and Karen McGarry note that ethnography "can and should be conducted in a variety of contemporary contexts."[16] Ethnographic methods "tread ways of carrying on and of being carried, of living life with others—humans and non-humans all—that is cognizant of the past, attuned to conditions of the present, and speculatively open to the possibilities of the future."[17] Ethnography also seems very appropriate to study two very different cultural groups coming together as ethnographic processes "focus on cultural complexity and global-local interrelations" that allow us to "understand, with a great deal of nuance and complexity, how cultures change and adapt to new situations."[18]

A post-modernist view of culture recognizes that culture is complex. Culture is not as unified or as culturally or internally consistent as once thought.[19] There is a diversity of opinions, styles, and ideas in social and ethnic groups. Power relations as well as cultural systems influence the lives of a community.[20] Moschella thinks of "culture holistically as the stories that guide our lives, the systems and symbols

---

13. Spradley, *Ethnographic Interview*, 4.
14. Spradley, *Ethnographic Interview*, 5.
15. Spradley, *Ethnographic Interview*, 5.
16. Mannik and McGarry, *Practicing Ethnography*, 4.
17. Mannik and McGarry, *Practicing Ethnography*, 4–5.
18. Mannik and McGarry, *Practicing Ethnography*, 6.
19. Moschella, *Ethnography as a Pastoral Practice*, 27.
20. Moschella, *Ethnography as a Pastoral Practice*, 27.

Research Methodology

that we believe in and live out through our actions."[21] This is a helpful perspective for generating a practical theology of welcome that admits that situations are complex as are human communities.

Spradley's ethnographic method focuses on participant observation and open-ended interviews that allow the researcher to gain implicit and explicit knowledge of culture gained through speech, both casual comments and lengthy interviews.[22] From recorded speech, the researcher makes inferences about what people in the community know, believe, and practice. This then leads to an understanding of culture bound reality, and an idea of how the people under study define the world.[23]

Language is critical in an inductive ethnographic study. It "permeates our encounters with informants and the final ethnography takes shape in language."[24] Researchers have to deal with two languages, the one of the informants and their own, even if the research setting is culturally familiar.[25] Spradley writes that ethnography involves discovery and description and that the description should be in the language of the informants, reducing the influence of translation competence as much as possible.[26] In order to accurately describe the informant's cultural reality, Spradley recommends a combination of descriptive, structural, and contrastive questions in a series of interviews with the informant. While descriptive questions begin the process by collecting a sample of the informant's language, structural questions lead to an understanding about how the informant organizes that knowledge. Finally, contrast questions "discover the dimensions of meaning which informants employ to distinguish the objects and events in their world."[27]

Analysis involves searching for "parts of the culture and their relationships as conceptualized by informants."[28] As this analysis involves

---

21. Moschella, *Ethnographic as a Pastoral Practice*, 27.
22. Spradley, *Ethnographic Interview*, 9.
23. Spradley, *Ethnographic Interview*, 11.
24. Spradley, *Ethnographic Interview*, 17.
25. Spradley, *Ethnographic Interview*, 19.
26. Spradley, *Ethnographic Interview*, 24.
27. Spradley, *Ethnographic Interview*, 60.
28. Spradley, *Ethnographic Interview*, 93.

symbols, it is important to define a symbol as "any object or event that refers to something."²⁹ This basis of symbolic meaning is the relationship between the symbol and the referent. This is where we derive referential meaning.³⁰ In Spradley's method, "the system of symbols that constitute a culture" becomes important.³¹ Spradley further identifies the process as more than a collection of symbols. The focus is on "the meaning of any symbol in its relationship to other symbols."³² This is the basis for the relational theory of meaning. Decoding symbols involves finding their referents, but more importantly, understanding the relationships that occur among the symbols.³³ We can then organize symbols into categories, which "serve to reduce the complexity of human experience."³⁴ Symbolic categories that include other categories are termed "domains."³⁵ As cultural knowledge is made up of many domains, the analysis involves determining and describing domains of cultural knowledge expressed by the informants. These domains and sub-domains arise from coding data obtained through the informant interviews and the resulting transcripts.

Moschella defines ethnography as "a way of immersing yourself in the life of a people in order to learn something about and from them."³⁶ In a congregational setting like WCRC, "ethnography can be practiced as a form of pastoral listening and care in the work of prophetic leadership."³⁷ Such research can fit into a model of a communal context that takes into consideration the "living human web of life both within and beyond the local community."³⁸ The advantage of ethnography as a pastoral practice is that it can bring a congregation into an "analogous

---

29. Spradley, *Ethnographic Interview*, 95.
30. Spradley, *Ethnographic Interview*, 96.
31. Spradley, *Ethnographic Interview*, 97.
32. Spradley, *Ethnographic Interview*, 97.
33. Spradley, *Ethnographic Interview*, 97.
34. Spradley, *Ethnographic Interview*, 98.
35. Spradley, *Ethnographic Interview*, 100.
36. Moschella, *Ethnography as a Pastoral Practice*, 4.
37. Moschella, *Ethnography as a Pastoral Practice*, 4.
38. Moschella, *Ethnography as a Pastoral Practice*, 5.

co-authoring process."[39] It can help pastoral leaders get a better feel for the undercurrents of congregational life and "help them navigate better in currents whose patterns they recognize and understand."[40] Ethnography as a form of pastoral listening can empower the congregation to find her voice and soul.[41] Moschella notes that, if this process goes well, the pastor and the congregation become co-researchers.[42] By employing this method, the anticipated outcome was that the Iranian newcomers and the longer-term English speakers would gain a voice within their communities and then together as the WCRC community as they continued to navigate the changes they experienced over the last three years. The narrative that resulted was an opportunity for the WCRC community to "recall its stories, its strength, its soul."[43] This will also give the leaders of WCRC an opportunity to understand the undercurrents and navigate them in life giving ways.

DATA GATHERING

The data collection phase began mid-January 2022 with MREB certification. The collection of data occurred from mid-January to the end of March 2022. I recruited nine informants for the research phase through an email from the church administrator. The email included two letters of information attached, one for English speakers and one for Farsi-speaking Iranians. The goal was to recruit eight informants with four from the English-speaking community and four from the Farsi-speaking Iranian community. I added one extra Farsi speaker to ensure that the minimum requirement of eight informants was met. This equal division of Farsi-speaking Iranians and English speakers was to allow for theological reflection on the host–guest dynamic of hospitality and to understand the movement toward mutuality. Another purpose was to understand the intergroup contact and social identity that were ongoing between the two groups. Pohl notes that there is a kind of hospitality "that keeps people needy strangers while fostering

---

39. Moschella, *Ethnography as a Pastoral Practice*, 6.
40. Moschella, *Ethnography as a Pastoral Practice*, 7.
41. Moschella, *Ethnography as a Pastoral Practice*, 13.
42. Moschella, *Ethnography as a Pastoral Practice*, 14.
43. Moschella, *Ethnography as a Pastoral Practice*, 18.

an illusion of relationship and connection."[44] Pohl also observes that "an important transformation occurs when people without power or status have the opportunity to be more than guests, when they, too, can be hosts."[45] Intergroup contact theory also posits that, as group interactions increase, prejudice and negative attitudes towards the out-group should decrease.[46] I designed the research sample to reflect on these questions.

The research involved weekly observation of two church events—the Farsi Fellowship meeting happening every Thursday evening and the Sunday morning service. Moschella notes that "when puzzling over questions of how a religious practice works in a specific context, it is helpful to go to the places where people engage in this practice and spend time there, seeing what you can see."[47] I informed the congregation of this observation process through a verbal announcement in the two gatherings and an email to the church membership list to give them an option to opt out of the study. Four individuals chose to opt out of the study, and I recorded the names of these individuals in my log. The four who chose to opt out were elderly English-speaking members who felt they could not contribute to the study. I took notes of interactions in these meetings as part of the ethnographic goal of collecting and analyzing both casual and intentional speech. I also kept a sample of the Sunday morning worship service bulletins as artifacts of the community and culture—for example, the Apostles' Creed which the officiating pastor reads every Sunday as part of the Lord's Supper celebration is printed in English and Farsi. Moschella gives guidance on such ethnographic observation, including beginning with a wide-angle view, taking everything in, and then moving on to people, actions, and interactions.[48] Context is also important as people may act differently in different settings.[49]

---

44. Pohl, *Making Room*, 120.
45. Pohl, *Making Room*, 121.
46. Ortiz and Harwood, "Social Cognitive Theory," 615.
47. Moschella, *Ethnography as a Pastoral Practice*, 68.
48. Moschella, *Ethnography as a Pastoral Practice*, 116–17.
49. Moschella, *Ethnography as a Pastoral Practice*, 117.

Research Methodology

One of the challenges of this research project was that the timeline of the data gathering (January to March 2022) coincided with the emergence of the Omicron variant of the COVID-19 virus, so both weekly meetings were held online for the initial part of the study. The congregation went back to in-person attendance on the last Sunday of February 2022 with a hybrid model of some in the sanctuary and some on Zoom. This made doing this research more challenging in a mixed virtual and in-person environment. When the church services changed to in-person, I also started attending in person following pre-approved COVID-19 protocols. Despite the easing of restrictions during the study, I continued with open-ended interviews of the informants virtually using the Zoom platform. Zoom interviews provided both convenience and good quality transcripts through Zoom recordings and the EnjoyHQ software program. I anonymized and checked transcripts and then uploaded them into MaxQDA Analytics Pro Student 2022 software for coding and analysis.

In sampling for interviews, I accepted volunteers on a first-come, first-served basis. In only one case did I not accept a volunteer because at that point I had more females than males. In that case, I waited for a male volunteer. As it turned out, six females and three males volunteered, mostly older adults reflecting the demographic of the congregation. The study involved more informants who were leaders in the church and people generally invested in welcoming and leading the Iranian community. There were two younger adults in the study. The oldest informant was seventy-four and the youngest was twenty-four. The average age of informants was fifty-one.

Questions were modified for English speakers and Farsi-speaking Iranians. For this reason, I attached two letters of information to the email sent to church members that included some sample questions for each community. The reason for the different questions was to explore the host–guest dynamic and to reflect on the context where the Farsi-speaking Iranians were new members of the congregation and the host members have been there for several years (although some English speakers were relatively new arriving in Canada during the last ten to fifteen years).

While some questions—such as describing the experience of welcome—were similar for both groups, I asked Farsi-speaking Iranians to explore the role of Iranian culture in their experience of welcome. If the informant had an Islamic background, I asked about the effects of this background on their spiritual growth. I asked the Farsi-speaking Iranians about their experience of immigration. I asked how it affected their experience of welcome. It became clear that support for immigration hearings was a very important part of being welcomed into WCRC. I specifically did not ask questions about the past life of Farsi-speaking Iranians in Iran due to the risk of re-traumatizing refugee claimants. However, if this information was voluntarily provided, it was recorded. I attached information on supportive counseling services through a church related agency to the follow-up email recruiting the informants for a second interview.

Moschella notes the challenge of ethnographic listening. The researcher must give up the role of expert and become a learner.[50] Ethnographic listening also involves tolerating uncertainty and suspending judgment. The ethnographic researcher must stay curious and allow for stories to be told.[51] The task of the researcher is to create "a space where new and honest speech can emerge in a community."[52] Such speech leads to an ethnographic narrative that in turn allows for theological reflection. Moschella observes that "narrative theologians claim that storytelling is the primary way in which human beings' structure and understand their experience of life."[53] Such a narrative can involve a "thick description" of the situation. Such a narrative is a detailed and interpretative description that conveys understanding of the deep meanings of the observations of the researcher.[54] It includes "the tacit import of gesture, word, or action in this particular context."[55] If done

---

50. Moschella, *Ethnography as a Pastoral Practice*, 142.
51. Moschella, *Ethnography as a Pastoral Practice*, 143.
52. Moschella, *Ethnography as a Pastoral Practice*, 143.
53. Moschella, *Ethnography as a Pastoral Practice*, 144.
54. Moschella, *Ethnography as a Pastoral Practice*, 197.
55. Moschella, *Ethnography as a Pastoral Practice*, 197.

Research Methodology

well, such ethnographic research is an opportunity to "co-author the future with the community and with God."[56]

DATA ANALYSIS

I analyzed recorded transcripts of interviews mainly using domain and taxonomic methods. Zoom recordings were downloaded into Enjoy-HQ to produce transcripts. I then went over the transcripts to anonymize the data as well as to correct mistakes. In some cases, I re-listened to the Zoom interview and corrected errors. This was important for informants for whom English was a second language. Once I produced accurate transcripts, I imported them into MaxQDA so that I could do *in vivo* coding to obtain the initial codes. In Spradley's method, these initial codes are termed "domains." Once I identified domains, it was then necessary to identify the most important domains of the study and then identify any sub-domains and the relationships between these subsets. Spradley recommends doing this through both domain and taxonomic analyses.[57] Moschella notes the challenge in working with ethnographic data in deciding how to "slice" the data so that the scheme of organization will help the researcher to think through the research question.[58] In this method, the codes and their organization emerge from the data and are therefore similar to grounded theory. While grounded theory is more inductive, Moschella notes that pastoral ethnography is usually abductive, combining both inductive and deductive reasoning.[59] She writes, "participant observation tends to lend itself to this kind of back and forth: your experience of a social setting works on you while you are working on understanding it."[60]

Spradley recommends using "Grand Tour" types of questions in order to get a general understanding of the culture and experience for the initial interview questions.[61] Structural questions follow (or can be asked concurrently) to focus on single semantic relationships (x is

56. Moschella, *Ethnography as a Pastoral Practice*, 255.
57. Spradley, *Ethnographic Interview*, 144.
58. Moschella, *Ethnography as a Pastoral Practice*, 170.
59. Moschella, *Ethnography as a Pastoral Practice*, 171.
60. Moschella, *Ethnography as a Pastoral Practice*, 171.
61. Spradley, *Ethnographic Interview*, 86.

a kind of y) as a main tool of analysis and to identity sub-domains.[62] Using descriptive, structural, and contrast questions, it should become possible to increasingly understand the culture of welcome through its different components identified by the domains and their subsets expressed by the informants.

While the interviewer usually begins with descriptive questions to identify domains, it is possible to build in structural questions to further define domains and their linguistic contents. I found that it was necessary to do analysis while the interview series progressed, to further define structural questions for the next interview.[63] Spradley's method helped me to understand the main domains and then to explore some of the domains more deeply. In all ethnographic research, there is a tension in exploring widely on the surface or going deeper into specific areas of the culture. Most ethnographers choose a compromise of some surface exploration and then deeper analysis of a few domains. It is important to note that the timeframe for this research was limited to three months so I had to make choices about what could be explored in the timeframe. Spradley notes that this balance of surface understanding and deeper investigation is one that ethnographers often strive to reach in their research.[64]

I began with open-ended interview questions seeking to understand the experience of welcome in the church. I asked about key people, experiences, and memories. I then moved on to the experience of welcoming the Iranian community and being welcomed if the informant was a Farsi speaker. I explored some of the benefits and challenges of welcoming so many members of the Persian community into the church congregation in the last three years from both perspectives. There was also an opportunity for informants to add any further information that they wished to add in subsequent interview sessions. As the research method involved a series of three interviews, I was able to analyze the transcripts between interviews and code for emergent themes and language around welcome. I then modified questions for

---

62. Spradley, *Ethnographic Interview*, 145.
63. Spradley, *Ethnographic Interview*, 145.
64. Spradley, *Ethnographic Interview*, 134.

the second and third interviews to understand better the use of specific terms used by informants.

For example, one informant expressed the need for time to help the congregation adapt to the many changes they were undergoing. In the second interview, we explored his use of the word "time." The concept of time seemed to be a positive aspect of adapting to change and growing into the new situation. On the other hand, in terms of "busyness," especially among members of the Iranian community, time was considered a challenge to welcome. Another informant referred to the sacrament of the Lord's Supper as being an important part of welcoming the other because it "transcends language." In the second interview, we were able to explore further how the Lord's Supper functioned at WCRC, especially in that it is celebrated every Sunday, which was not a usual practice for Christian Reformed churches. One informant expressed how important his baptism was to him and all of the hugs he received. These two experiences became a domain under welcome through the sacraments and led to theological reflection around Eucharistic hospitality and baptism as initiation.

Fairly early in the interview phase, it became clear—this was confirmed by participant observation—that there were two avenues of welcome at WCRC. The first was through several key English-speaking leaders at WCRC. The other avenue of welcome was through the leaders of the Farsi Fellowship. The Iranian couple who led the group were the first Iranians to come to WCRC and were themselves welcomed warmly by certain WCRC church leaders. Once settled, this couple then brought many Farsi-speaking Iranians to WCRC. This growth happened slowly over time and was called "slow trickle growth" by an informant. This insight helped to form the beginning of a taxonomy of welcome based on these two avenues. It became possible to put other domains of welcome under these two main categories. Another important decision on the part of the Iranian leaders of the Farsi Fellowship was to remain as one church and not to hold a separate church service in Farsi. The Thursday evening meetings, while mostly in Farsi, functioned more as a Bible study and teaching time and not as a time of worship. Worship continued to be reserved for Sunday morning. This was an important insight because some sub-domains rested under both avenues and pointed to the unity that was part of the WCRC story.

From this initial insight, the taxonomy grew and was further defined through structural questions and further descriptive questions in subsequent interviews. I obtained further information in the third interview with structural questions, some contrast questions, and even final descriptive questions such as "Tell me a story of an important event in your experience of welcome into the WCRC congregation." I found that the informants in this research study did not use such unique terms as the "tramps" or "jug" that Spradley describes in his study. The informants in my study did use certain terms such as "time," "singing," "volunteering," "anxiety," "translation," "slow trickle growth," and "legacy members" that needed further explanation, description, and comparison to fully understand the meaning of the terms as used in the WCRC context. Four of the informants spoke English as a second language. One informant spoke through a translator. Four informants spoke English as a first language.

The informants helped to identify intentional practices and rituals involved in their experience of welcome, and in welcoming others. I also sought to understand the process of inclusion and discipleship that continued after the initial welcome for those who chose to stay at WCRC and become members. Informants pointed to a culture of welcome at WCRC that has developed over many years but became particularly apparent in the face of congregational decline and the providential welcome of the Iranian newcomers. It is important to note that some of the leaders of WCRC intentionally worked to prepare the church to be a welcoming congregation in the face of challenges such as an aging congregation and a loss of identity with their former Dutch culture and history of immigration.

ETHICAL CONCERNS

Moschella encourages the ethnographic researcher involved in pastoral listening to bring reverence into research relationships: "Reverence is a profound respect and regard for the dignity of persons and communities who all us to see so much of themselves."⁶⁵ Before beginning this research project, I received an MREB certificate. Procedures for recruitment included ensuring that informants provided consent and that privacy was protected. The church administrator who was the information content holder sent out an email to all members of the church with the letters of information for recruiting informants for interviews. Interview informants then contacted me to set up Zoom interviews.

Informants gave oral consent for recording at the beginning of the online interview sessions. In one case, an informant requested after the first interview that I not record the second and third interviews, so I switched to taking notes. I documented the oral consent of informants in an oral consent log. For the participant observation component, an opportunity was given to the congregation to opt out. The names of the four individuals who opted out were recorded, and they were not included in any way in the study. The translator signed an oath of confidentiality. I gave the informants the opportunity to withdraw from the study at any time with no penalty. No incentive was given to participate. I made efforts in the design of this research project to hear from both communities within the church.

In any study of this nature with two different communities, it is possible to prioritize one over the other, in this case the host over the guest. The host generally has power over the guest and more control over the situation. The guest is in a more vulnerable position. The guest on the other hand can sometimes feel paternalism in the welcome of a host in a powerful position. In this study, it became evident that the Iranian guests did not want to remain guests forever. Such dynamics were part of the tension of both challenge and blessing in the roles of host and guest in the WCRC context. Sometimes the roles were reversed, and the guests became hosts, and the hosts became guests. This became an important part of the theological reflection. I found myself at times identifying with both the host culture (my community) and the guest culture (as I am an outsider although with the privileges of a pastor).

I found it easier to relate to the English speakers describing CRC culture due to the ease of communication in English. I do not have

---

65. Moschella, *Ethnography as a Pastoral Practice*, 87.

a Dutch heritage and so am sometimes myself a guest. In interviews, I struggled to understand the Iranian worldview and found the responses of the Iranian informants were shorter and less descriptive. I believe this was due to the challenge of English as a second language because Persian culture is a culture rich in storytelling and poetry. In one case, the challenge was doing interviews through a translator. It was helpful that the interview series included three sessions, allowing rapport to develop with the informants. Moschella observes that ethnographic accounts are limited by time and space, and so is a snapshot, influenced by the researcher's attitudes, inclinations, and motivations for doing the research.[66] For this reason, I included journal reflection and recorded my thoughts and emotions.

I made efforts to balance gender in the study as much as possible with MREB consent requirements. The interviews involved six females and three males. Three of the females were Farsi-speaking Iranians, and three were English speakers. Two of the males were Iranians, and one was an English speaker. I wondered why it was easier to recruit female volunteers. Could it be that females play a greater role in the process of welcome at WCRC? I made efforts to balance language and to allow all voices to be heard, in both English and Farsi, and to allow for those who did not feel comfortable sharing in English to have a translator present. Those who volunteered to be in the study were more competent in English than some of the other members of the Farsi Fellowship. It became clear in the study that Farsi-speaking Iranians who were better English speakers had more opportunities to volunteer in the church and take on leadership positions. This gave them a higher status in the church and more power in the community. This may have also led them to volunteer for this study more quickly.

REFLEXIVITY

For the ethnographic researcher, reflexivity is important as it meets the ethical demand for self-awareness.[67] It is important to reflect on "what bothers us, causes us to judge, or otherwise captures our attention."[68]

66. Moschella, *Ethnography as a Pastoral Practice*, 28.
67. Moschella, *Ethnography as a Pastoral Practice*, 106.
68. Moschella, *Ethnography as a Pastoral Practice*, 106.

Research Methodology

Throughout the data collection phase, I kept a journal and wrote down my thoughts and reflections on the experience of participating in the congregation and interviewing informants on a regular basis. For example, I may have been more subconsciously open to Iranians with better English skills. I also functioned as a part time teaching pastor and preacher during the period of data collection, preaching three times, once in the Farsi Fellowship, and twice during the Sunday morning worship service. This added an additional dynamic to my relationship to the congregation in that I was not just an observer but also a teacher. During some Farsi Fellowship meetings that I attended as an observer, I was asked to share my opinion as a pastor, and the need for translation slowed down the meeting. This need for translation created some tension in the Farsi Fellowship. While I felt uncomfortable and would have preferred to be just an observer, I realized that the Iranian community often welcomed and gave honour to pastors and Westerners who were their guests.

At one point in the study, I became conscious of some conflict in the Farsi Fellowship. I did not want to take sides or create more conflict through my research. I reflected on the fact that I was not comfortable with conflict, yet I observed that the Iranian community had a culturally different method of communication that was more energetic, engaging, and sometimes combative. At times, this made me feel uncomfortable, which I attribute to a combination of my personality and my Western culture. Personal reflection was helpful for me to work through some of these feelings.

I also spent some time reflecting on how this research project functions both as host—to the church congregants and the informants—and as guest, a relative newcomer to the congregation who needs to be accepted in order to build rapport and, as Moschella encourages, to become a co-author of the study alongside the congregation.[69] I continue to reflect on the role of the researcher as both host and guest in a congregational setting. I could not have done this study without the gracious support of the council of WCRC and the leaders of the Farsi Fellowship.

---

69. Moschella, *Ethnography as a Pastoral Practice*, 255.

SUMMARY

Using Spradley's method, ethnographic data were collected through nine informants and through participant observation in two weekly services at WCRC. Each informant participated in three one-hour interviews involving descriptive, structural, and contrastive questions to understand better the culture of welcome at the church and specific practices and rituals of welcome and inclusion. Interview transcripts were coded for emerging domains and sub-domains to understand key themes and categories functioning in the congregation. Efforts were made to balance the number of English and Farsi speaking informants (host–guest) and to balance gender as much as possible. Ethical concerns were considered, and a reflexive process was described. The analysis of the data obtained through interviews and observation is the focus of the next chapter.

Chapter 4

Discussion of Data

INTRODUCTION

I obtained data from twenty-seven transcripts that resulted from my interviews with nine informants. I coded these transcripts for domains and sub-domains. Transcripts were generated by the EnjoyHQ program and uploaded into MaxQDA except for informant No. 9 who asked to not be recorded for the last two sessions.[1]

The COVID-19 pandemic was an important limitation, which will be noted at the beginning of this analysis. Once this is covered, I described the major domains or codes that arose from the interview data. My focus was on the prevalence of references and other comments that pointed to the importance of these domains and subdomains. I also compared and contrasted the data with sources in the literature review. I will reserve theological reflection for chapter 5. I will conclude with a brief section on reflexivity and a summary.

Fetterman notes that ethnography "is iterative, building on ideas throughout the study."[2] He also notes that analysis is about finding your way through the forest and that the "fieldworker must find a way

---

1. Informant No. 9 felt that his answers would be more natural if he was not being recorded. In this case, I took notes, and those notes became the transcript that I uploaded into MaxQDA.

2. Fetterman, *Ethnography*, 93.

through forest of data, theory, observation, and distortion."[3] In order to help find a way through the forest, codes were grouped together to represent similar categories of welcome, such as people, experiences, practices, challenges, and other categories as they arose from the data. Wherever possible, I endeavoured to let the informants set the categories through specific references to church leaders, events, sacraments, and other areas of congregational life. I kept track of common references that informants made in response to certain questions.[4] I compared informants' responses with my own impressions of visiting WCRC services and Farsi Fellowship meetings. I structured observations and interviews to help understand and respond to the research question on the challenge and opportunity of welcoming a group of people from a different cultural and ethnic background. These newcomers could be considered strangers at the door and completely unknown to the long-term members of WCRC. Where possible, I listened for references to God and the informant's experiences and reflections of God at work in their individual stories and in the life of the congregation.

I analyzed the data in ways to understand the development and ongoing practices, rituals, and attitudes around a culture of welcome, hospitality, and inclusion of the Farsi speaking members of the church. The data reveal insights into the culture in the church and the embodied theology of hospitality functioning there. Was the welcome of the Farsi newcomers a special event limited in time in the life of the church or the result of a long legacy of welcome?

As the research progressed, through descriptive and structural questions, other domains such as guest–host dynamics, challenges to welcome, inclusion, and the use of the sacraments became part of the discovery. The main domain that arose from the data was the importance of a small group of five English and two Farsi speaking leaders who were mentioned often by informants as very welcoming. Another important domain included the decision to be one unified church together rather than split into English and Farsi speaking communities. This decision allowed the process of welcoming by the English and

---

3. Fetterman, *Ethnography*, 93.

4. MaxQDA software was helpful in coding and grouping the responses to the questions asked.

Discussion of Data

Farsi leaders to continue to the present and to allow for the study of the inclusion of the Farsi speaking newcomers into the church.

I examined the experience of welcome of both English- and Farsi-speaking Iranians. I sought to identify specific practices of welcome. Through the interview process, it became clear that the sacraments were important to welcome. Many baptism services that had occurred over the last two years were important to the welcome and inclusion of the Iranian newcomers. The leaders of WCRC had also decided to initiate a weekly Lord's Supper service, which would be an unusual practice in the CRC denomination. This decision was made before Adel and Parmida, the first Iranian couple, started to attend and clearly contributed to the culture of welcome.

I asked informants how welcome progressed to inclusion at WCRC and how Iranian newcomers moved from guest to host. Guest–host dynamics is an important part of a theology of hospitality. This became a specific domain in response to an English-speaking informant who shared that the Farsi-speaking Iranians at WCRC "did not want to remain guests forever." I wanted to examine if attitudes and perspectives had changed in each group through contact with another group and asked a specific question related to this to see if social contact theory was a factor in the unified church. One informant talked about the Farsi-speaking Iranians being a gift to the congregation, so I explored how each was a gift to the other. My overall goal was to identify the existence of a culture of welcome at WCRC. While there were many different responses, I tried to focus on the main domains that arose from the interviews. I noted these dynamics again when I observed them in my participation at WCRC over the research period. Through these domains, I hope to tell the story of welcome at WCRC. I edited quotations from informants for clarity without changing the original meaning relayed during interviews. I changed names to protect identity and ensure anonymity.

A sample list of questions can be found in the appendix. As the methodology allowed for semi-structured open-ended questions, I added new questions through the series of three interviews. I followed the ethnographic methodology of Spradley's developmental sequence. Interview questions started with descriptive questions, such as

"Describe your first experience of welcome at WCRC," in the first round of interviews. The second round involved structural questions, for example, "What are five characteristics of a welcoming person?" or "What are the social activities that you have been involved in at WCRC?" The third round involved some contrast questions like "How is an Iranian welcome different than a Canadian welcome?" I found contrast questions the most difficult to formulate, and the informants had the most difficulty understanding and responding to such questions. In the second and third rounds, I also began to explore questions like "How is the Iranian community a gift to WCRC?" or "How is WCRC a gift to the Iranian community?" I observed that many of the informants referred to the welcome at WCRC as "warm." So, I started asking what they meant by a "warm" welcome. The following chart illustrates the most common domains that arose from the interviews.

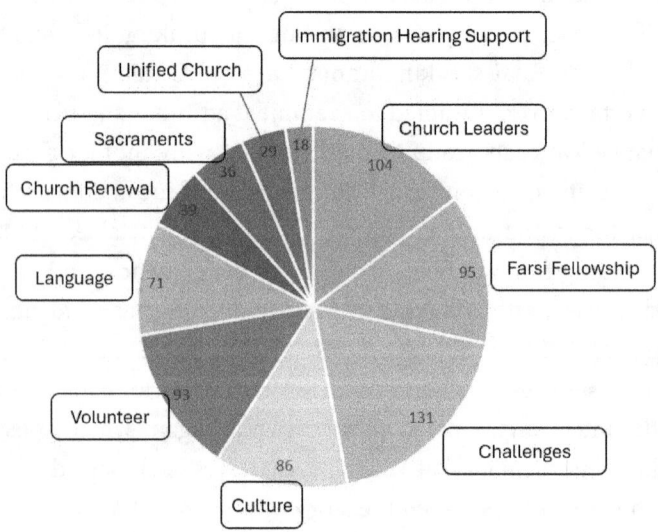

Figure 1. Prevalence of Domains

MISSING DATA AND LIMITATIONS

A few observations point to the potential for missing data and limitations of this study. It is important to note this this research project occurred after two years of the COVID-19 pandemic and during the

Discussion of Data

fifth wave surge caused by the Omicron variant. I noted both references to the pre-COVID-19 experience of welcome as well as experiences of welcome on Zoom. While the experience of welcome remained consistent during the switch to online church, the practices of welcome changed. Zoom especially affected the cultural appreciation for physical touch so valued by the Iranian community.

The research informants were mostly leaders in the church, many presently in formal leadership roles, or having leadership experience in past roles. Four out of the nine informants did not hold an official role in the church at the time of the interviews. It is possible that the informants represented a group of people already invested in hospitality and eager to explore this subject further. I also interviewed eight out of the nine informants in English and only used a translator for one informant. This may point to the confidence of Iranian English speakers in volunteering for a study of this nature and to the possibility of bias on the part of selecting informants who are already very committed to hospitality and welcome and who have very positive views of the other group. As it was important to ensure consent, I accepted people who volunteered and contacted me on a first come basis. Only in one case did I not select a volunteer in an effort to balance gender. This may have meant that I did not hear from Iranian newcomers who did not speak English well or who did not hold a leadership role in the church. Future investigation could be done into the more marginalized members of the congregation. More females than males volunteered to be informants. With these limitations in mind, the following results are categorized by domains.

ENGLISH- AND FARSI-SPEAKING CHURCH LEADERS

In the first round of interviews with informants, it became apparent that two groups of leaders were instrumental in welcoming newcomers at WCRC. The first group consisted of five English-speaking church leaders who were particularly welcoming. The second group was the Iranian couple who lead the Farsi Fellowship. This Iranian couple Adel and Parmida were themselves warmly welcomed by the English-speaking leaders. Adel and Parmida over time invited other Farsi-speaking Iranians to join the congregation. This growth, referred to by one informant as "slow trickle growth," led to the Farsi Fellowship growing from a few newcomers to over one hundred and fifty at the time of this writing. One informant had performed over one hundred baptisms in the last two years. The welcome of the Farsi-speaking Iranians by the Farsi leaders was reinforced by the continuing warm welcome of the English-speaking leaders, both in supporting Adel and Parmida and in welcoming new Farsi-speaking Iranians themselves. This contributed to a cycle of welcome reflecting the existence of a culture of welcome at WCRC. This discovery occurred through responses to the question "Please describe your first experience of welcome at WCRC." I addressed this question to both English- and Farsi-speaking informants.

In my experience of visiting WCRC in person when some COVID-19 restrictions were lifted, I found myself talking at the door with one of the church leaders. I personally experienced the warm welcome expressed by the informants and so the informants' responses were reinforced by my own participant observation. This points to the reliability of the observation.

I noted that this welcome by leaders went back several years. English-speaking informants who had first come to WCRC between ten and twenty years ago identified individuals who warmly welcomed them. One of these individuals was now only able to attend Zoom church from a bed, but she had left a legacy of welcome that influenced the church. One informant referred to her when he said, "The community people call her a community lady. She is a connecting person. She goes into the community and talks to people and that is what she does whenever a new person comes." Another English speaker said, "And this voice said hello, and I turned around and it was Fenna." In this way, a pattern of welcome developed over the years that became particularly needed at the time the Iranian couple Adel and Parmida first came to WCRC looking for a new church home. This legacy of welcome continued into the present through four leaders on the WCRC council who continued to welcome newcomers after the pastor left for another church. This pastor, to whom I have given the name Aaron, was active in practicing welcome and hospitality at the time the Iranian couple first attended WCRC. This small group of leaders, both English- and

Discussion of Data

Farsi-speaking Iranians, became catalysts of welcome or what we could biblically call "people of peace" as referenced in Luke 10:6.

It is important to place this welcome by church leaders in the context of congregational decline due to an aging population at WCRC. The congregation was established in 1963 during post-World War II immigration that led to the growth of Christian Reformed congregations in Canada. Over the years, the population declined as members became elderly and moved to Christian Reformed seniors' residences and nursing homes such as Holland Homes in Brampton, Ontario. At the same time, the cost of real estate in the Willowdale neighbourhood of Toronto was increasingly out of reach for young families. This contributed to the decline of the congregation. Just before Adel and Parmida first attended WCRC, there had been a significant loss of members to Holland Homes and another seniors' residence in Aurora, Ontario. The congregation was down to around sixty to seventy members with very few children in 2017.

In 2017, the pastor began to worry about the congregational decline with the departure of a few couples to Holland Homes and another seniors' residence in Aurora. At the time, he felt that God gave him a vision of Jesus walking with the two disciples on the road to Emmaus. One informant shared, "Pastor did a lot of praying about it, and he felt that he was getting the message, 'Follow the road to Emmaus,' and some of us just really didn't understand what he was talking about, but he just kept saying, 'You know, the congregation will grow, and we need to be faithful to God's calling and to God's word.' And then the congregation started to grow."

It became clear that Parmida and Adel had a special role to play as not only persons of peace welcoming many from the Persian community but also as bridges between the two cultures, English-speaking Canadian culture and Farsi-speaking Iranian culture. Not only did they help Iranian newcomers find their way to church, but they also helped Canadian members understand Iranian culture. It is important to note that Parmida is a gifted translator and that helped in bridging cultures between the two communities. I personally observed her ability to translate for the Farsi-speaking community and for the English-speaking community on a number of occasions during the participant observation phase. Aldiabat, Alsrayheen, Aquino-Russell, Clinton, and Russell note the difficulties of integration into Canadian society for Syrian refugees. The authors found that Syrian refugees needed time to know and understand Canadian culture while Canadians needed time to learn about the background and experience of newcomers.[5] Parmida and Adel had an important role of both helping the Iranian newcomers to learn about Canadian society and helping the Canadians to learn about the background experiences and culture of the Iranian members. Aldiabat and his co-authors note the importance of cultural sensitivity in the provision of health care to Syrian newcomers to Canada.[6] Adel and Parmida were able to provide culturally sensitive care to the Farsi-speaking newcomers and to work with the English-speaking leaders in helping them to become more culturally sensitive. One English-speaking informant noted that time was needed to adjust to the new situation in the church for both communities. Aldiabat and his co-authors also noted the importance of time for Syrian newcomers to understand Canadian culture and to adapt.[7] Together the English-speaking and Farsi-speaking leaders were able to work together towards being one unified church together.

One other point in this process was the slow rate of growth of the Farsi-speaking population of the church. It started with Adel and Parmida and then increased slowly over the past three years to the point where there are approximately one hundred and fifty Farsi-speaking Iranians associated with the church. The growth rate was slow in the sense that a large number of Farsi-speaking Iranians did not come to the church at the same time but came individually and in families over the three-year period. In writing about his experience with welcoming Karen and Chin refugees into his church, Carmen found that the rapid change was one of two significant challenges leading to members feeling overwhelmed.[8] This was not the case at WCRC, allowing the congregation to adapt and change at a slower pace. The changes still

---

5. Aldiabat et al. "Lived Experience," 486.
6. Aldiabat et al. "Lived Experience," 484.
7. Aldiabat et al. "Lived Experience," 486.
8. Carmen, "I Was a Stranger," 13.

Discussion of Data

presented challenges, but the slower rate of change did help to smooth the process.

ONE UNIFIED CHURCH TOGETHER

The Iranian leaders of the Farsi Fellowship along with the council of WCRC made a conscious decision to be one unified church. There are Korean-speaking and Russian-speaking congregations and then English and Farsi lettering for the combined WCRC. The fact that the English- and Farsi-speaking Iranians came together to form one church is significant. Aaron, the then-pastor, approached the Iranian couple Adel and Parmida to ask if they would like to form a separate congregation of Farsi-speaking Iranians meeting in the church. They declined this offer. They had come wanting to be part of the congregation and to receive pastoral care and support in the context of the whole church; so they felt that, in whatever way God led the congregation to grow, they would remain together. Parmida recounted the story:

> He [the pastor] said, "Would you want to have a separate Farsi ministry or Farsi fellowship?" But you know, for us churches, the body of Christ, and for us to be church, is to become one with, I don't want to refer to Willowdale as the host, but maybe even at that point, they were our host, and we were probably the guest or the stranger they had welcomed, but we felt that God was calling us to do church together with Willowdale.

Other informants also responded to the importance of being one church together. One Farsi speaking informant Shadan said, "Because it is a mixed community, I must be sharing. No, it cannot be all Farsi or all English. I think it nice to share." Nikoo, another Farsi-speaking informant, said, "So, we gather and we pray every time for this unity. This is the best thing that we have in this church, you are right." Edward, one of the English-speaking informants, said, "We are one church with two kinds of speaking groups, but we are all one church."

Carmen, describing the experience of Burmese refugees and their integration into his church, notes three principles that guided the welcome and inclusion of the newcomers, two of which apply to WCRC. There was a conscious decision to include the newcomers in the life, leadership and decision making of the church. Further, they decided on unity and openness to each other to form one church rather than three.[9] WCRC also made these kinds of decisions that helped to unify the church and focus on being one church together for worship on Sundays and other important social events and small groups despite language and cultural barriers. Becoming and staying as one church then opened other opportunities to share spiritual gifts with each other leading to a number of sub-domains.

How Are the Farsi-Speaking Iranians a Gift to WCRC?

A question related to being one unified church together was "How are the Iranians a gift to WCRC and how is WCRC a gift to the Iranians?" This question developed from a comment made by an English-speaking informant Heather early in the interview series when she commented that the English-speaking members, especially the leaders, were realizing that God was bringing them a gift. The gift to the congregation was the presence of Iranian newcomers. This realization happened early in the process of Iranian newcomers coming to WCRC but was part of the movement to be hospitable and to start observing the Lord's Supper on a weekly basis. The most common references related to the gift of the Iranian community to WCRC were church renewal, inspiration, and energy.

Church Renewal

Church renewal was referred to forty times. From the English-speaking side, it was clear that the Iranians brought renewal to the church. Iranians brought with them children and young people. They brought a desire to learn more about Christianity with many questions and much interest. Diba, a Farsi speaking informant, observed that the number of children and young adults had increased quite a bit as the Iranian community grew. Many of the Iranian newcomers are new Christians and they bring curiosity and passion with them. The number of baptisms in the congregation, surpassing one hundred and twenty, was a sign of this new vitality and energized the whole congregation. Edward described

---

9. Carmen, "I Was a Stranger," 13.

Discussion of Data

the effect of the Farsi-speaking newcomers in this way: "Although it may be Farsi [-speaking people] are keeping the church alive through what might be a declining period a little bit as well, I think it's just keeping the energy and providing new energy and honestly making the world a better place." The Iranian newcomers also bring a belief in the power of prayer and give testimony to many answered prayers. This was something that I observed in a service focused on God's miracles, including testimonies of answered prayer. Von Kaehne notes that, in his Persian ministry context in the UK, a similar vibrant prayer ministry was occurring among the Iranians including a "stunning trust" in the power of prayer.[10] This was observed at WCRC.

"Inspiration"

"Inspiration" was the most common term used by English-speaking informants. Inspiration was mentioned thirteen times. Edward described the effect of the Iranian newcomers, "It's really touching to see and hear from new Christians because it's not that I have forgotten how it's just a reminder. It really is. And you know, it makes you think, because some of the stories that I've heard is, you know, they've literally risked their lives and the lives of their families." Norma, an English-speaking informant, said, "Many of our Farsi members wake up in the morning excited to find out what the Bible verse will be, that will come on telegram, and are excited about coming to the Farsi Fellowship because they are going to learn about Jesus." Heather said about the Farsi-speaking Iranians, "Some of them listen to our sermons two or three times a week. I don't know a Dutch [Canadian] person who does that." One reference to inspiration came from a Farsi-speaking Iranian Diba who was inspired by Farsi-speaking Iranian leaders on the church council.

"Energy"

"Energy" was another term used to describe the change in the church; it was noted seven times. Energy was both a gift and a sign of church renewal. Edward described the influence of the Iranian newcomers, saying, "They are energy." Sofie, an English speaker, described the energy

---

10. von Kaehne, "Iranian Diaspora Ministry," 444.

added by the newcomers, saying, "They just want to help. It creates a sense of, you know what, we want to do something, give us some work to do. Can I help?" Sofie added, "You know, a person like me, I feed on that energy, too." One Farsi speaker Yara also perceived this energy when he said through the translator, "And when he said that it started to change, I think he means, it became active, more energetic."

How Is WCRC a Gift to the Farsi-Speaking Iranians?

For Farsi-speaking Iranians, the key sub-domains in which WCRC was viewed as a gift included providing a safe space for the Iranian community and providing support for the refugee hearing process. They also looked to the long-term English-speaking members of WCRC as models for living the Christian faith, as a family replacing the family they had left behind in Iran, and as supports for learning English and Canadian culture.

Safety and Security

Farsi-speaking Iranians often come from Islamic contexts where identifying as a Christian can pose risks, and they bring some of those concerns with them to Canada. Farsi-speaking informants mentioned the need for safety fifteen times. The leaders of WCRC protect and provide security to their Farsi-speaking members by not mentioning last names in any publications, even if for just local use. The leaders allow only one person to take photos at baptisms and other special events. During Zoom calls, particularly for Farsi Fellowship meetings, sometimes people call in by phone without an identifier. Adel and Parmida check to ensure that everyone is identified, and once identified, they ask the caller to introduce themselves. Shadan emphasizes the importance of this, saying, "So, feeling safe is important, it is an important thing for Iranian immigrants feeling safe in the church." Nikoo said, "They wanted there to be no film, no video. And it's right, because we have the connection back home with country and we see people still are getting arrested by the government and they are in jails because of their face." Heather recognized this need when she responded, "I think Willowdale has done a good job of recognizing that we have to protect some

Discussion of Data

of these people. They make a commitment to Christ and there's fall out in Iran if it gets into the wrong circles." Referring to the inclusion of refugees, Langmead mentioned the importance of "creating a safe and welcoming space for those who are different from each other, especially for those who are strangers in the dominant culture."[11] It is evident that WCRC has provided such a safe space.

Refugee Hearing Support

Another way that WCRC has been and continues to be a gift to the Farsi-speaking Iranians is through support for the refugee hearing process. For the Iranian newcomers, many of whom are refugee claimants, support around the immigration hearing process was very important. They cannot remain in Canada and pursue careers and studies unless they become protected convention refugees. Von Kaehne notes the importance of this support in his ministry in Glasgow, Scotland. His policy was to baptize all who request it and not to question motives, while supporting asylum applications and giving testimony in court.[12] This support for asylum applications—or in the Canadian context, refugee board hearings—was mentioned eighteen times. Shadan talked significantly about the support she had received around her immigration hearing from the Farsi Leaders Adel and Parmida as well as an English-speaking leader Connor. She said, "Connor, Adel, and Parmida were on the phone asking what is happening. Connor is sending emails. Twenty-four hours answering when it is close to the court. They are supporting I can say, twenty-four hours, asking, what do you want?" Shadan went on to describe some of the stress that she experienced around her refugee hearing that went from eleven in the morning to six or seven in the evening, "I was feeling that I couldn't see anything, because I didn't eat anything, I didn't drink anything." One of the Farsi-speaking Iranians, Nikoo, directly addressed the importance of the immigration hearing letter and that this is a major motivator for the Farsi-speaking Iranians to come to church in the first place. Three of the English-speaking informants noted this reality also. Edward summed up the feelings well when he said, "It's just another requirement of the

11. Langmead, "Refugees as Guests and Hosts," 42.
12. von Kaehne, "Iranian Diaspora Ministry," 445.

Canadian government, but it helps, right? I would hope that for them, being part of the Christian family is more important, but I get it." Like von Kaehne, the leaders at WCRC decided to baptize the new Iranian believers who professed faith in Christ without questioning their motives. They provided letters of support and encouragement for the hearings when requested.

Role Models

As many of the Iranian newcomers are new Christians and many of the long-term members are elderly Christians, it was mentioned that the English-speaking members became like role models for the Iranians. They found both inspiration and guidance in living the Christian life by observing these older English-speaking members. Shadan said, "I think their patience is very important, and we are learning from them, of course, in their Christianity, in their beliefs we can learn from them a lot because they read Bible word by word and they know a lot that we can learn from them." Nikoo said, "You know, when you see someone, in the Bible, it says that you can know a tree through the fruits. So, when you go, you get to know the strong Christians in faith with that manner."

Family

Identifying as a family was also an important quality of being a part of WCRC. This was mentioned twenty-one times. Farsi-speaking informants mentioned that, as an immigrant community, they felt like the Farsi Fellowship was a family. Parmida suggested that this was intentional from the beginning: "So, this is one of the most innovative approaches that our Farsi Fellowship has had in terms of bringing people together as a family." Nikoo, referring to the immigrant experience of many of the Farsi-speaking Iranians, said, "Now we have literally no one, except for my family church, we have no one here." Nikoo was referring not only to the Farsi Fellowship but also to the entire WCRC church community. She continued, "Willowdale is my real family, Pastor Sinclair, because they are supporting me in many ways." Families support each other, and an important aspect of this at WCRC is the

Discussion of Data

support that people receive as newcomers to Canada. English-speaking informants noted this family-like quality for Farsi-speaking Iranians as well. Edward said, "It also gives them not only a place of worship but also a place of trust that some might call home and that not everyone has a biological family due to their separation from Iran." Diba said, "I think it affects how we think of our place, because it is like we entered into a family."

Learning English and Canadian Culture

A desire to learn English and Canadian culture in the context of the WCRC congregation was expressed by several Farsi-speaking Iranians. This sub-domain was referenced seventeen times. Shadan, concerning the Farsi-speaking Iranians, said, "They start to learn a little bit because they want to make a connection with their brothers and sisters in church." Nikoo noted that the Farsi-speaking Iranians are also interested in having their children integrate in Canadian society. Edward shared his perspective of the needs of the Farsi-speaking community: "What I hear is that these folks want to learn the language and learn what it means to be a Canadian, learn to skate, or just to go to Tim Horton's and talk." Norma said that WCRC has provided a "safe and welcoming place to learn about us—about Canadian culture and Canadian Christian culture."

EXPERIENCE OF WELCOME

In asking informants about their personal experience of welcome, some informants used certain terms that were more affective such as "warm" and "kind." Other informants described what an experience of welcome should be like or described efforts to provide such a welcome. This question was directed to both English speakers and Farsi-speaking Iranians. The word most often used to describe the welcome received at WCRC was "warm." The following chart captures some of the more common responses.

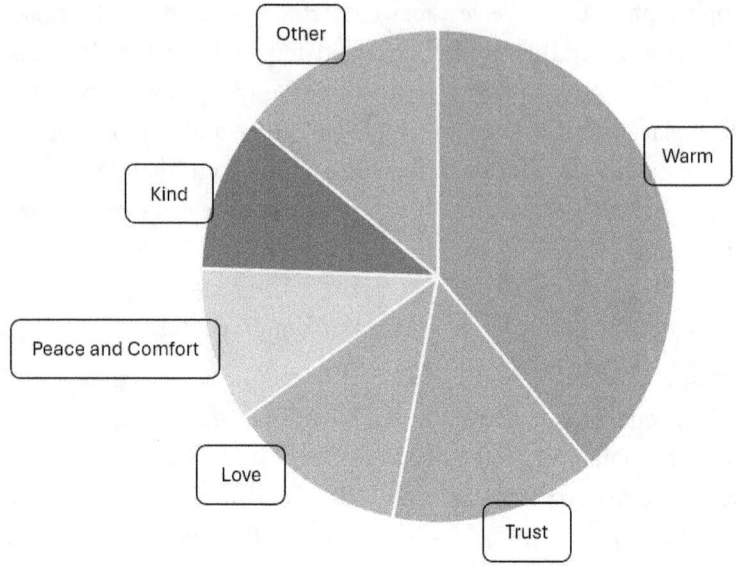

Figure 2. Affective Domains

Warm

Parmida, the first Iranian who came to WCRC with her husband Adel, experienced this warm welcome by a small group of English-speaking leaders at WCRC, which led them to stay. They were also looking for pastoral care, and WCRC reminded them of the church they had attended in Iran. About three to four months after their arrival at the church, Adel had a stroke and received frequent pastoral care by Pastor Aaron. This pastoral care solidified their membership at WCRC. Since Adel and Parmida had been involved in a ministry to Farsi-speaking Iranians before coming to WCRC, during the recovery period after the stroke, they continued to contact Farsi-speaking Iranians and invite them to WCRC. In this way, the Farsi-speaking community grew over time thanks to the invitations by Parmida and Adel. Much of this growth occurred during the COVID-19 pandemic while the church was meeting over Zoom.

Informants referenced a "warm welcome" nineteen times in interviews. Informants referenced a "warm culture" three times. I explored what they meant by the word "warm" in the second and third round of interviews with some of the informants. Yara described a warm welcome as the result of the love and affection of the Farsi Fellowship leaders Adel and Parmida. This reference also reinforces the importance of the leaders in this experience of welcome. Yara continued to explain that, through the affection of these leaders, he became attached to the church and learned what it meant to be a Christian. Another informant Sofie described a warm welcome, saying, "Somebody comes to you and says, 'Hi, hello, welcome to Willowdale. What's your name? Where are you coming from? Come and have a coffee with us. You should meet this person and connect'—that kind of thing." Sofie also contrasted a warm welcome with a "cold" welcome by saying, "People don't even see you as new people. They don't want to have eye contact with you. They leave you alone and you feel awkward after the service."

Nikoo shared that she came with the expectation that a Canadian welcome would be a "cold" welcome. But when she came to WCRC, she experienced many people coming up to her and being happy to see her. She recounted, "Imagine you're coming to a place for the first time, and then many people, like more than ten people, families, they come to you, and they are happy to see you, and they ask you to go to them, and they invite you." Nikoo also related how two church leaders asked her if she needed anything—a ride, or anything. One of the leaders invited her to her house for a "beautiful meal." Nikoo was invited to use her gifts on the worship team. Nikoo likes to use her gifts to sing in Farsi and she was given the opportunity to do so.

Trust

Trust was expressed by informants six times, and this points to the importance of trust and safety for the Iranian newcomers. One informant simply said, "I think trust is key." One English-speaking informant attributed this to the background of many of the Farsi-speaking Iranians coming from an Iranian background where a lot of suspicion resulted in a need for them to experience trust. Yara, in referring to his church experience, said that being accepted was important because, when you come to a new environment with lots of fears and anxieties, "you are looking for a place you can trust."

Love

Love was described by Parmida as an important part of their ministry to Farsi-speaking Iranians. She described their ministry to Farsi-speaking Iranians as sharing the love and being friendly. Describing the Farsi-speaking newcomers, she said, "They need love, and they need care, and they need a listening ear to listen to their needs. And you need a friend, a friend in Jesus." Adel also expressed God's love to the newcomers by taking them with him on fishing trips.

Peace and Comfort

Two Farsi-speaking Iranians and one English speaker described feeling comfortable as an important part of their experience. This was significant because the original couple, Adel and Parmida, felt welcomed at WCRC, which in turn encouraged them to become part of the congregation and continue their Farsi ministry there. Yara linked peace and comfort together. The translator explained, "What he loved about it was the physical presence in the environment, which gives him a lot of peace and comfort." Yara went on to mention three more times that he felt a special sense of peace and that he was always happy to go to church.

Kindness

Two Farsi-speaking informants mentioned the importance of kindness. Shadan mentioned the kindness of Adel and Parmida as "making me want to come here," pointing also to the importance of the welcome of church leaders. She also mentioned the importance of equality and kindness. Yara also mentioned the importance of kindness in his experience of welcome at WCRC.

Other Feelings

Other feelings were expressed by individual informants. Shadan described joy in the church by contrasting the experience at WCRC with her experience with Islam in Iran. She said, "Their singing is with crying for that Mullah who is dying, or that Mullah who died or that prophet, there are things like that for just crying and killing themselves." She added, "I believe that God wants [us] to be happy, not crying." Sofie emphasized the importance of honesty in the experience of welcoming newcomers to the church. Yara also mentioned honesty. He said, "You know that, without fears, you can sit and receive the truth, and the truth will be shared with you honestly." In speaking of the characteristics of a welcoming person, Yara said, "cheerful and honest." Parmida identified the need to belong as important in the experience of welcome for Farsi speaking newcomers. Heather emphasized being open to the work of the Holy Spirit.

PRACTICE OF WELCOME

The responses point to the importance of practice in welcoming and including people from a different cultural and ethnic background. Informants spoke of an observed set of practices and attitudes that led to the growing community of Farsi-speaking Iranians at WCRC. One story from about ten years ago tells of a man who would consistently stand by the door and greet everyone with a handshake, not letting anyone pass by without a greeting and a handshake. This example pointed to the importance of a physical presence at the door of the church. Greeting at the main door was a general practice at WCRC, and Sophie said, "They're very welcoming at the door. So that everybody who enters the door, I think, will feel the same sense of warmth regardless of who you are, which I experienced, and I always wanted to welcome them and invite them to a worship service." Other welcoming practices were noted but with fewer references. Informants mentioned making eye contact twice, once in the context of greeting and the other in the context of the Lord's Supper. Smiling as a part of the welcome experience was mentioned by Shadan and by Edward. Home hospitality was mentioned five times. Edward mentioned that he had three or four people asking him if he had a place to go at Christmas, and if not, "They invited me to their houses." Nikoo shared that part of a warm welcome for her was the invitation to visit a leader's home. She said, "She took me home." Nikoo was translating for a new Farsi-speaking couple, and the same leader said to her afterwards, "You know what? I want to welcome them to my house."

WELCOME TO INCLUSION

One of my questions involved asking how people who are welcomed are included over the long term. Another way of framing this question was exploring how WCRC helped guests move into the role of hosts. The responses of the informants pointed to multiple ways of helping people feel included in the congregation and move from guest to host. This included the decision to be one unified church, which led to a context of worship in a combined setting of English- and Farsi-speaking Iranians on Sunday morning, mainly in English with some parts in Farsi and a weekday meeting mainly in Farsi with some limited English translation if English speakers were present. This weekly meeting on Thursdays became the main source of discipleship for the Farsi-speaking Iranians. Another significant discipleship resource was the after-sermon discussion on Sunday mornings in English and Farsi with translation. The responses of informants made it clear that the servant-leadership style of Adel and Parmida was effective in helping people feel included. This also involved encouraging the newcomers to participate in volunteer activities in the church. Another important factor for including the Farsi-speaking part into the full life of the church was being elected to ordained leadership as elders and deacons.

Servant Leadership

Adel and Parmida had a clear philosophy of involving the community of Farsi-speaking Iranians in their decisions as was noted by several of the informants. This servant-hearted and democratic approach contrasted with other Farsi ministries in Toronto that tended towards authoritarian leadership. For example, Shadan had tried one other church and did not like the authoritarian leadership style there. She said, "When you come to class, they force you to do something. And I was like, 'What's happening here?' Here is that you are doing the same thing that Mullah is doing in Iran." In contrast, she said this about her experience of coming to the Farsi Fellowship, "They listen to me, you know, it feels very good because you feel that the person who's, I can say the leader they're in Farsi Fellowship, they are leading, they are listening to you. I feel it's giving very good feeling for you because I didn't experience that

Discussion of Data

in the previous church." Adel and Parmida had committed to a servant-leadership approach in their Farsi ministry. Parmida expressed it in the following way: "We want to do it in a communal way. Come and let us do it together." She continued in the next interview, saying, "If they have the passion, we want them to be involved. And it's not always about being right or wrong, Pastor Greg, we want to support them by even making mistakes and learning from that mistake in their journey." I had the impression from some of the Farsi-speaking informants that this was not typical in Iranian churches. Shadan spoke about this when she said about her experience in another church: "A Persian guy who was there was the leader. You feel like you are a slave, and there is a boss, and you are talking to a boss there." Shadan also compared her experience of a more authoritarian leadership style in church with her experience of Islamic leadership in Iran: "And I was like, what is happening here? Here you are doing the same thing that a Mullah is doing in Iran." She then contrasted this approach with the approach of Adel at WCRC: "Then I started to talk with Adel, and he was very welcoming. I told him I am writing the Bible as poetry and he and Parmida encouraged me to continue to write it." Nikoo observed this in the Farsi Fellowship group: "They are more than welcome to do whatever they like, like to act, to be themselves, not to have to be under restrictions."

Volunteer Opportunities

An extension of this philosophy of servant leadership included engaging members of the fellowship in activities such as the Farsi Radio or special events such as Knock Days as soon as possible. Shadan shared that she was initially involved in Knock Days, a special outreach initiated by the Farsi Fellowship to members of the congregation who were isolated due to the pandemic. Adel and Parmida also initiated a Persian Internet-based radio station both to outreach and to give members of the Farsi Fellowship opportunities to volunteer, learn new skills, and be discipled in the faith. Shadan mentioned her involvement: "I was with the team, and we had Knock Day, at the beginning I was a volunteer for Knock Day as well. But after a while I started radio, the radio for the church. Right. And I was the person who was in charge for radio." Adel and Parmida looked to support the special gifts, abilities, and interests of their individual members. For example, Shadan shared that she had special gifts as a poet and was putting the Bible into Farsi poetry. She was encouraged by Adel to pursue this, and it was the first time that she had been encouraged in a Christian setting to use her gifts of poetry. She said, "I was starting to write Bible in poetry because I'm a writer in Persian and writing stories and poetry in Farsi." She said, when she told Adel, "That is even because I wasn't encouraged from the previous church, I was saying very shy that, you know, I'm writing Bible as poetry, [Adel] said 'Wow, you are doing a great job. Send me some of your poetry.' I said, 'Okay.'"

Ordained Leadership

One of the important decisions of the WCRC council was to invite Farsi-speaking Iranians into ordained leadership positions such as elders or deacons. This was not without controversy, however, as Adel and Parmida wondered whether the Farsi Fellowship had a sufficient number of mature disciples ready to take on ordained leadership. The English-speaking leaders were pushing for Farsi-speaking ordained leaders. So, the hesitation was on the Farsi-speaking side. There was the added challenge that many of the Farsi-speaking Iranians were still learning English and the council wanted Farsi-speaking Iranians who were competent in English. Adel and Parmida were the first to be ordained as elders. It was originally proposed that they be called "shepherds." But this did not fit well into the Christian Reformed Church polity and Church Order guidelines, which only acknowledge pastor, elder, and deacon as official roles. Due to this, they were instead ordained as elders. There did not appear to be any controversy around ordaining women elders and deacons. This was an accepted practice at WCRC, and the Farsi-speaking Iranians embraced it.

The next year, Nikoo was ordained as an elder as she had sufficiently good English language skills. Eventually, other Farsi-speaking Iranians were ordained so that currently all three pastoral care wards of the church have Farsi-speaking Iranians. This has benefited the whole community, as the Farsi-speaking Iranians tend to be more sensitive to Iranian cultural needs and can provide ministry in the Farsi language when necessary. Nikoo shared that she had a lot of support in learning the role of elder. She also noted that she had some Farsi-speaking Iranians and some English speakers on her pastoral care list. Nikoo commented, "I really enjoy doing it, Pastor Greg, not only the Farsi Fellowship people I'm doing, I'm serving, that makes me enjoy it. It makes me like comforted, but also some of the English speakers as well." Edward also noted this change: "Our Farsi folks are also getting involved, much more now in leadership, whether it's elders, deacons, or different committees, like the intercultural group." Sofie also noticed the intentionality of including Farsi-speaking Iranians: "I think leadership has really worked and pushed hard to include mature Christian converts into leadership."

Having Farsi-speaking ordained leaders has presented some challenges. Norma shared, "We have Farsi-speaking deacons who are still struggling with how it all works." Norma also commented, "They're an asset because they can speak for their culture and their people." This is reminiscent of Carmen's experience with Burmese refugees and their integration into the full life of the church, including leadership and decision making.[13] Nikoo shared that being ordained as an elder did create some jealousy among the Farsi-speaking Iranians. She felt that not everyone respected her in her role. She commented on the challenge of being ordained: "They would not accept me as an elder because maybe I'm young, not very young, but to them, I was one of the youngest people there. And then I was one of them."

GUEST-HOST DYNAMICS

The Farsi Fellowship hosted the Iranian newcomers while functioning as a guest within the host WCRC congregation. This dynamic posed both opportunities and challenges. One image to help explain the dynamic would be to picture a smaller lake (the Farsi Fellowship) draining into a larger lake (WCRC). Despite being committed to one system, there was not always a smooth flow from one to the other. Some English speakers attended Farsi Fellowship events but mainly the flow was from the smaller lake to the larger lake. Then barriers to welcome and inclusion function like dams on the river between them in this analogy.

---

13. Carmen, "I Was a Stranger," 13.

Sometimes barriers such as language prevented flow back and forth. Sometimes it was the level of maturity and Christian discipleship. This was true for the development of Farsi-speaking leaders in the congregation, especially to ordained roles. For example, Parmida said, "The Farsi Fellowship has for sure become a host for people who feel like they are strangers, who feel now like they know the Lord." Parmida admitted that, in the larger WCRC context, "Sometimes it does not feel that you are a host." Heather repeated something that she had heard from a Farsi speaker in the intercultural group: "Farsi folks say we don't want to be guests forever. We want to contribute." This comment expressed some of the frustration that Farsi-speaking Iranians felt in wanting to be accepted fully as part of the congregation. Heather went on to say that the solution was for the English speakers to sometimes be uncomfortable so the Farsi-speaking Iranians could feel more like hosts. One comment reflected the importance of inviting Farsi-speaking Iranians into ordained leadership in the church. Norma said, "I would certainly think that people on council don't feel like guests."

IMPORTANCE OF THE SACRAMENTS

Informants noted the importance of both the weekly practice of the Lord's Supper and the many baptism services held at WCRC as important practices in welcoming the Iranian newcomers. Although related to both welcome and inclusion, it seemed significant enough to the informants to require a separate section.

Baptism

Baptism was significant in the Farsi Fellowship. Regular baptism services were scheduled to accommodate the number of baptisms taking place at WCRC. This was a new phenomenon for the church. These services were scheduled as separate services due to COVID-19 restrictions. In reflecting on these baptism services, Sofie notes three benefits of these services: (1) we are tied together because we all remember our baptism; (2) they remind us of the nations coming together as a fulfilment of God's promise; and (3) baptisms are a strong testimony of God's mission. Sofie noted that baptism services point not just to the

Discussion of Data

hospitality of WCRC but ultimately to the hospitality of God: "So, it's a very strong testimony. I think of God's mission. In a sense, it's the hospitality of God, isn't it? It's God who is showing hospitality to all of us."

For several of the informants, baptism was an occasion where they remembered and would continue to remember into the future. Yara shared that it was the people around him and their warm hugs that made that day special: "I wanted to share that the day we were baptized was a very special day and we were hugged, and you know, it was really the warmth of the people around us and the way that they hugged us. It just made an image in my mind that always stays with me."

Leaders at WCRC developed a training class to prepare for baptism but did not delve too deeply into motivation for baptism. The leaders wanted to build trust and admitted, however, that it was difficult to understand people's motives, which were often mixed and complex. They trusted that God was leading the new disciples towards this event. They also felt that, despite the possibility of mixed motives, people were hearing the gospel and getting Christian teaching on Thursday evenings and Sunday mornings. For example, Nikoo said, "I think it is good to know more than 90 percent of the Farsi-speaking people come only for immigration but most of them are tired of the religious things in life they have been practicing." She went on to say, "From my perspective, if from this 90 percent even if 20 or 30 percent find God, find Jesus, I think it's perfect." This is like Peter von Kaehne's experience in the UK. He said that their policy towards baptism was to baptize all who requested it and not to question their motives while supporting asylum applications and giving testimony in court.[14] This was the approach of the WCRC leaders in holding baptism services (usually separate events due to COVID-19 restrictions)—WCRC did not question their motives. Several Farsi-speaking informants noted how important the immigration hearing support was to them. Testimonies of those baptized were published in English for use within the church. The purpose of this was to share the stories of spiritual growth, sometimes including stories of suffering and persecution, so others in the congregation could be edified.

---

14. von Kaehne, "Iranian Diaspora Ministry," 445.

Lord's Supper

The leaders of WCRC decided to move to a weekly celebration of the Lord's Supper before Adel and Parmida first came to WCRC. Pastor Aaron had wanted to move in this direction as part of becoming a more welcoming congregation, and this proved to be an important part of the welcome at WCRC. As Heather observed, weekly Lord's Supper transcended language and communicated welcome to new members and helped to welcome the Farsi-speaking Iranians: "They, Pastor Aaron, and some of the leadership would have said weekly Lord's Supper is one way we can communicate non-linguistically a welcome to the expanding table." This change was part of the Holy Spirit's movement to prepare the congregation to receive the new Farsi-speaking Iranians. Heather continued and said, "And when they were finally able to say the reason is that the Spirit is inviting them into weekly communion to prepare them for all these Farsi-speaking Iranians that are coming. And so, I think the other benefit of this is to actually wake up and say, are we partnering with what the Spirit is doing?"

A number of the informants, both Farsi and English speakers referred to the tactile physical aspect of the Lord's Supper. Regarding his experience of weekly communion, Diba said, "Every Sunday I remember the taste of the small sip that we take from the small containers."

The Lord's Supper celebration at the end of the service is preceded by a recitation of the Apostles' Creed printed both in English and in Farsi. Sophie recounted how the Lord's Supper served as a practice and ritual that both welcomed and transcended linguistic barriers in her experience. She related a story of visiting a church where she did not understand the language, but she did recognize the practice of the Lord's Supper. She recounted, "Once you experience that you are the one person who does not understand what is going on in the community, and then when you experience something that you understand without understanding a word, and that was during communion, then you can kind of flip that around and see how meaningful that is to make all of us one at the table." This made her more sympathetic to the needs of the Farsi-speaking Iranians.

Discussion of Data

CULTURE OF WELCOME

One of my goals was to investigate if the welcome of Iranians at WCRC was part of a wider culture of welcome or *habitus* in the church. Ammerman and Farnsley define the culture frame of a congregation as the ways that a congregation has invented to be together in a unique way.[15] Ammerman notes that because culture is complex, it is helpful to focus on one aspect of a culture. Ammerman writes, "It is easy to get overwhelmed by the complexity of a culture, and your task will be made easier if you develop a focus that will help narrow your work."[16] In this research project, the focus was on a culture of hospitality, welcome, and inclusion. Through the responses of informants, it became clear that the welcome of newcomers at the church went back many years and at least two individuals were identified as important people in the experience of welcome at WCRC before 2010. It also became clear that welcome at WCRC went beyond the welcome at the door into the community through special events such as Knock Day and other initiatives. Norma related how one WCRC leader was instrumental in welcoming her at church and even through encounters in the community. She related one incident, saying, "But you don't expect people who you don't know, and who don't know you, to stop you in the grocery store. That's like an extra level of being welcomed."

One of the questions that came up related to the small number of very gifted and motivated leaders that supported a lot of the hospitality at WCRC. Did this mean that a small group of gifted and motivated leaders were driving the welcoming culture? I posed this question in an interview to Nikoo, and she responded that a group of Sunday school leaders had mentored her and helped her to feel welcome in that setting. I had not explored the children's ministry at that point, so it appears that the welcome is indeed part of a wider culture that is particularly evident in the seven leaders who were mentioned often in interviews. Another informant responded by saying, "If you just come one time you are going to love it. The church family, the older people, they are so welcoming and kind." Edward commented, "There was a

---

15. Ammerman and Farnsley, *Congregation and Community*, 15.
16. Ammerman, "Cultural and Identity," 83.

particular woman at the door who welcomed me, not only that first day but from then on really, the people in the pews were welcoming." This highlights that the welcome at the door was repeated in the sanctuary and in church events.

Ammerman notes that a congregation's culture is often observable in their rituals. She notes rites of intensification and rites of passage.[17] WCRC has both. The Lord's Supper functions as a rite of intensification in the culture of welcome. The Lord's Supper ritual, preceded by a reading of the Apostles' Creed in English,[18] increases the intensity of "the group's commitment to its shared values and meanings."[19] For Ammerman, rites of passage "are transition events that mark changes in an individual's life or changes in the life of the congregation."[20] Baptism services function in this way for the Iranian community. This also includes profession of faith and certificates of welcome. One Iranian newcomer Shadan, who had been baptized at a previous church, received a certificate of welcome that made her feel very welcome. She said, "Here in this church they have a welcome certificate. I like it. Actually. It was showing that you are a member of our church and welcome." While the focus in a congregational study is the worship service, other groups in the church can reflect a culture and identity according to Ammerman.[21] This is the case for the Farsi Fellowship on Thursday evenings. Such groups often function as support groups as well as forums for study and discussion. The Farsi Fellowship not only provides this kind of support but also makes space for welcome and inclusion through introducing new members and allowing guests to attend. Inclusion happens as some of the members of the group lead different parts of the study and discussion. In some of the sessions I attended, different members were asked to present different chapters from Genesis, and then the discussion was led by the main leader Adel.

---

17. Ammerman, "Cultural and Identity," 86.
18. It was also printed in Farsi.
19. Ammerman, "Cultural and Identity," 86.
20. Ammerman, "Cultural and Identity," 87.
21. Ammerman, "Cultural and Identity," 87.

Discussion of Data

Ammerman notes that such shared activity "creates an additional base on which the culture of the congregation can be built."[22]

CHALLENGES TO WELCOME

Despite the many positive responses received by the informants referring to the warm welcome and hospitality at WCRC, it became apparent that there were many challenges to welcome and that some instances when WCRC was less than welcoming. Webb notes that it is important to note negative examples as well.[23] It is easy for both the informants and me, as the researcher, to become invested in portraying a positive and welcoming image of the church, while ignoring any negative examples that arise in the interviews. It is also important to understand the challenges to overcome in the ongoing process of welcome and inclusion at WCRC. The chart below outlines the main challenges identified, including language, cultural differences, Islamic influence, busyness, resistance, and anxiety.

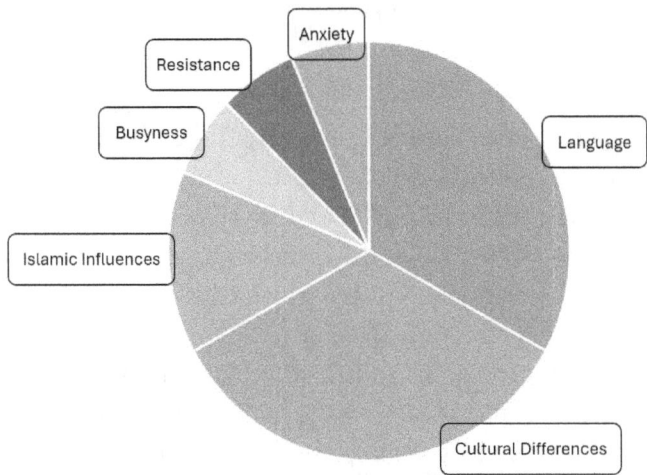

Figure 3. Challenge Domains

---

22. Ammerman, "Cultural and Identity," 87.
23. Webb, *So You Want to Do a Qualitative Dissertation?* 158.

Language

One of the main challenges to welcome and inclusion is the language barrier. Many of the newcomers to WCRC are new to Canada, and their English skills are limited. The older English-speaking members do not speak Farsi. Some of the elders and deacons have learned a few words, but their ability to converse in Farsi is non-existent. The push in the church is to learn English to become more involved in the congregation and take on leadership roles. Parmida's translation gifts have helped this process. Parmida is the main translator and does much of the translation on a Sunday morning and at the Thursday evening Farsi Fellowship meetings when English speakers are present.

Farsi-speaking Iranians with better English-speaking ability were able to take on leadership roles at WCRC more quickly, and this led to some jealousy in the Farsi-speaking community. Parmida spoke of this challenge: "They felt that there is some kind of favouritism happening that, *Well, if somebody is speaking English, I'm not*. So that person is preferred. And that's one challenge."

Cultural Differences

The mixing of two very different cultures and the challenge of understanding each other were present at WCRC and continues to be a hindrance to welcome and inclusion. Cultural differences as a category was referenced eighty-seven times, which makes it a significant theme—the importance of church leaders was the only theme that was referenced more frequently than this one. Some of the informants referenced an intercultural team of English- and Farsi-speaking members that met for several months to discuss some of the cultural differences in the two communities. This led to some recognition of cultural differences. Four cultural differences mentioned by Farsi-speaking informants included the following: (1) the Iranian cultural concepts of *ta'arof* ("extreme hospitality"); (2) patron–client power dynamics; (3) a shame-and-honour worldview; and (4) competition and jealousy. These are cultural concepts that may not always be understood by the English-speaking community. Heather also mentioned cultural traits that are specific to Dutch Canadian culture and how they contrast to Iranian culture.

Discussion of Data

Ta'arof

Oksnevad defines the Farsi word *ta'arof* as "a verbal dance between an offeror and an acceptor until one of them agrees."[24] This leads to an "aversion to telling the truth, particularly when it is shameful."[25] Parmida shared that she believed that *ta'arof* was part of the Iranian community accepting hospitality from Western hosts. I observed *ta'arof* operating to some extent in the interview process. The Farsi informants were very hesitant to find anything wrong with WCRC in recounting their experience of welcome or to be critical in any way. When I had asked if they had any experiences of unwelcome, Diba thought about the question until the next interview and then offered feedback on ways to improve the radio project and suggested a fund to support social activities and "to help the group integrate into Canadian society."

Patron–Client

Iranian culture is very status oriented. Parmida thus noted that a chair of a church council had power, and so there would be a desire to become a client of that dominant power. The nature of the refugee board process means that a letter from the church council chair is beneficial to applicants during their refugee hearing. This reinforces the patron–client dynamic in the church and the power of the chair of council as patron and the Farsi-speaking Iranians as clients.

Shame and Honour

Shame and honour are a part of Iranian culture that presents unique challenges for the deacons of the church as they minister to the Farsi-speaking community. One example was shared of an Iranian member who had a large debt, much larger than the deacons could provide for through their benevolence fund. This individual was able to solve his problem through *culturally appropriate ways*. Nikoo pointed out that, because of shame and honour, people were not always able to share the problems they were facing in life, even with their families. She

---

24. Oksnevad, *Burden of Baggage*, 59.
25. Oksnevad, *Burden of Baggage*, 59.

continued and said, "Like if I have a problem, I feel ashamed to talk to my mother or my father about it."

Competition and Jealousy

Parmida noted this tendency as a challenge of leading the Farsi Fellowship and maintaining unity—she said, "We have a culture, if I may say so, of competition, comparison and gossip because of the corrupt government that they have been dealing with (in Iran)." Oksnevad notes this challenge to unity in his research into Iranian Christian communities. He writes that especially gossip is prevalent in the Iranian church made up of Muslim-background believers and that it is a source of conflict. When he asked his informants how gossip in the Iranian church compared to gossip in the non-Iranian church, he was told it was "more intense and pervasive."[26]

Dutch Canadian Culture

Within the Christian Reformed Church in Canada, there remains a subculture that combines Dutch and Canadian cultures. While it is hard to pinpoint, some references were made in interviews about "Dutch" people, specifically in contrast to Iranian culture. One example provided was differences in grieving rituals after the death of a loved one. Iranian people mourn for a specific period of time and receive much more attention during this period, whereas in the Dutch Canadian culture of WCRC, initial concern would be expressed, but it would quickly dissipate. This could lead to different expectations for pastoral care. Another example referred to the general concern for appearance of Iranian women. Dutch Canadian culture downplays wearing make-up and jewelry. This became an issue during baptism services when the liberal application of water became a problem for some of the Farsi-speaking women who were concerned about their appearance. Heather referenced a cultural difference around giving gifts. Dutch Canadian culture places less emphasis on gift-giving, whereas Iranians place significant importance on this practice, especially when they are guests. When an Iranian is invited over to a home, cultural expectations will

---

26. Oksnevad, *Burden of Baggage*, 79.

Discussion of Data

influence them to bring a gift for the host. A Dutch Canadian person would not think about this.

Islamic Influences

Another challenge that was noted was the ongoing influence of the Islamic culture that many Iranians have grown up with, even though many were no longer practicing Muslims at the time of their conversion. Some Farsi-speaking Iranians described themselves as cultural Muslims. One of the effects of this was a rejection of authoritarian leadership style. An Islamic background also led to some misunderstandings of Christian theology and practice. This pointed to a need for discipleship and maturity before taking on leadership roles. Diba described his Islamic background and conversion to Christianity with the analogy of learning the guitar incorrectly and having to re-learn it. This is much harder, he said, and it takes more work to learn correctly. Adel and Parmida, the leaders of the Farsi Fellowship, were sensitive to the discipleship needs of former Muslims. Adel, who had been raised in an Islamic home but converted to Christianity as a young man, was sensitive to these issues.

Busyness of the Iranian Community

Busyness was expressed as a challenge for the Farsi speaking community in general. Many of the Farsi-speaking Iranians worked long hours in order to get established in Canada and to send money back to Iran. Many were also working at furthering their education or obtaining professional credentials. This meant that, between work, studies, and church activities, it took a high level of organization to be able to participate in church activities and opportunities such as the Farsi radio. Some of the Farsi-speaking Iranians have moved away from North York due to the high cost of housing. Many continue to attend WCRC, but transportation becomes an issue. Diba explained, "I work construction many days from 8 in the morning to 7 in the evening." Sofie, observing the community, said, "So, people are studying, working a menial job here and there driving Uber. They're just so busy." Nikoo, too, observed, "They are very very busy with making up life all over again from the beginning." She also noted some of the logistical challenges that the Farsi-speaking community faces: "I don't remember exactly, but it was very hard for some of those people to come from their work to church, and then afterward to home because many of them didn't even have a car."

Anxiety and Resistance

Some informants noted anxiety in the English-speaking community at WCRC. This group has experienced change over the last three years due to the increasing number of Farsi-speaking Iranians and the added stress of the COVID-19 pandemic. Norma expressed it this way: "What I hear in bits and pieces is that Iranians have taken over the church. There is a sense that there is too much Farsi spoken. I think it is because there are so many people, there are more Iranians in WCRC." Norma also noted that the English-speaking community is not growing and that being online due to COVID-19 restrictions have hidden the true numerical growth of the Iranian community. She concluded, "I think people will be shocked when they come into the church and see that the Farsi people are equal with the non-Farsi-speaking Iranians." Heather also observed that there is "a lot of anxiety in the system" and that there is a perception that "the Farsi-speaking Iranians have taken over." She concluded that the problem with anxiety is that it makes us "uncreative and kind of dumb." This hampers the ability of the church to adapt to this change in creative ways.

Another challenge to welcome noted among the English-speaking community is resistance. Parmida felt that the leaders of the church both insisted on hearing her opinions but at the same time *resisted* her opinions. The English-speaking leaders struggled with accepting suggestions from the Farsi-speaking leaders. About the resistance, Edward said, "There may be pushback, there may be resistance, but the change is happening anyway. And change is happening in an appropriate way." Heather observed that some of the English-speaking members were not open to changing and adapting to this new situation. She commented, "I think there is a real tenacity that comes out of the builders that are still there to say, you know what, you can change after I am gone but I don't." Some of the resistance is related to language issues and could thus be placed under the domain of language. For example, Heather commented, "It's how much Farsi the English folks have to put up with." She also said that, for an aging congregation, it is challenging: "It's unfortunate but it's that old age, 'Don't mess, Don't move my cheese,' this is how I am used to it."

Social contact and identity theory helps to explain the origins of the perceived anxiety. Ortiz and Harwood note that anxiety is high in intergroup settings, especially when there are unclear expectations for group interaction. This anxiety is reduced through increased intergroup contact.[27] One of the challenges for WCRC that prevented intergroup contact was the pandemic, ongoing throughout the research phase of this book. While it was clear that, before the advent of COVID-19 restrictions, coffee time after church allowed for the mixing of the two groups and positive interactions, this was impossible while the church met on Zoom. Some of the informants mentioned positive interactions, however. For example, Norma remembered a Farsi speaking girl explaining the Iranian New Year's celebration to her at a special event. Ortiz and Harwood point to the importance of intergroup friendship in overcoming anxiety in intergroup interactions.[28] Vezzali and Stathi encourage cooperation to achieve goals together and institutional support to achieve increased positive intergroup responses. Cooperation results in cognitive dissonance as the intergroup interaction diverges from expectations in positive ways. This cognitive dissonance leads to positive change.[29] One would hope that increased exposure with the Farsi-speaking Iranians, especially as COVID-19 restrictions are lifted, will continue to lead to cognitive dissonance and positive change in the English-speaking community at WCRC.

EXPERIENCES OF UNWELCOME

Two episodes came up in interviews that pointed to an experience of unwelcome. In a study of this type, it is important to look any negative outcomes in order to understand the whole experience of the Iranian community. The first experience came from Norma who related

27. Ortiz and Harwood, "Social Cognitive Theory," 616.
28. Ortiz and Harwood, "Social Cognitive Theory," 628.
29. Vezzali and Stathi, "Extended Intergroup Contact Hypothesis," 116.

a situation of refugee sponsorship that was less than enthusiastically embraced by the congregation. About seven or eight years ago, an Iranian family was sponsored by a Christian Reformed church in Sarnia, Ontario, Canada. This family really wanted to settle in Toronto. A call went out to the Toronto churches to help this family move to Toronto and become established. After repeated requests by the deacons at the time to the membership of WCRC, most of the work fell to Norma to help this family. She said, "Somehow our church wasn't very helpful, either. I kept asking people, but I asked them as a group. Can anybody, on Sunday morning, help me? And nobody came forward." In discussing this episode with Sofie, she wondered if, as one family of Farsi-speaking Iranians in an English-speaking congregation, they did not find enough connection with the congregation due to the language barrier. Later, when Parmida and Adel came, they came with good English skills and did not ask too much of the congregation in terms of support. They were able to make a connection with the leaders and then began to slowly attract other Farsi-speaking Iranians. This helped the congregation to adapt to the newcomers over time and resulted in a more positive outcome with the later experience of welcoming Iranians.

The second experience of unwelcome was shared by Yara. He was part of a group of Farsi-speaking Iranians who had been nominated to serve on the council of WCRC, but in the end, the council felt that their limited English language skills would limit their ability to serve on the WCRC council and so their nominations were rescinded. Yara shared that he felt very sad about how it turned out.

EFFECTS OF SOCIAL CONTACT AND IDENTITY

I was curious to find if the presence of Farsi-speaking Iranians had changed the attitudes of the older English-speaking members in the church and if the Farsi-speaking Iranians had any changes of attitudes towards Canadians. Social contact theory states that prejudices should decrease in contact with a group of a different ethnicity and culture. This proved to be the case, although my investigation of this was limited to one question related to changing attitudes. Norma stated that she found the Iranians to be very warm and welcoming, as opposed to previously seeing Muslims as harsher and cold natured. This was

Discussion of Data

before her exposure to the Farsi-speaking community at WCRC. To quote Norma, "I think that the thing that has surprised me is that, that warmth and somehow I thought, I think of the Muslim culture is not, not, not being warm and loving." Norma had been exposed to Iranian culture seven years earlier when the church helped with a refugee sponsorship. Norma had become familiar with the needs of Iranian refugees before the Farsi Fellowship was started at WCRC. This means that Norma had previous experience with Iranian culture. It is interesting that the English-speaking informants that I interviewed were positive in their view of the Farsi-speaking Iranians. The informants did have significant contact with Farsi-speaking Iranians. It is possible that those who volunteered for the interviews were more active and open to learning about new cultures. Dixon and Rosenbaum point out a limitation to contact theory, arguing, "More prejudiced individuals avoid contact with minorities limiting its effect."[30] Individuals who volunteered for this study would not fall into this group of more prejudiced individuals. It is possible that this study does not include the perspective of those in the church who might be more prejudiced.

Social identity theory would point to the importance of a "superordinate identity." In interviews, it became clear that informants saw themselves first as children of God and then as members of WCRC. This reinforces the importance of being one unified church together. Abrams and Hogg point out that social identity forms around "individual knowledge that he/she belongs to certain social groups together with some emotional and value significance to him/her of the group membership.[31] While Farsi-speaking informants receive a lot of support from the Farsi Fellowship, they are committed to the WCRC community because of the opportunity to learn English and Canadian culture in a supportive environment. This has emotional and symbolic significance for the Farsi-speaking members and supports their process of identity transformation. Regarding the need to learn English, Shadan commented, "It's very good because we are living in the English-speaking country, right? The language here is English. If people around us just speak Farsi all the time, you will not start to learn English right?"

30. Dixon and Rosenbaum, "Nice to Know You?" 261.
31. Abrams and Hogg, "Introduction to the Social Identity Approach," 2.

Yara said, "Potlucks they had on Sundays, they were able to taste, you know, like they were Iranians, the other group were Canadians, they were tasting each other's food." Captari and her co-authors advocate for direct contact and genuine closeness and meaningful relationships with refugee populations, which will lead to mutual dependence.[32] There is evidence of the development of such meaningful relationships in the WCRC congregation, particularly before COVID-19. Shadan said, "It's very good that we get to know some Canadian friends, and we can get, you know, more familiar with their culture." Norma referenced a friendship with a Farsi speaker, saying, "We've become friends, you know, in a sort of way. She's been in my home to work on something together, and I've been in her home to work on something together." Diba noted that, while he enjoyed making Canadian friends on Sunday, he had limited contact with English speakers during the week.

GOD AT WORK

In listening for embodied practices and rituals of welcome, I tried to keep an ear open for references to how God was perceived to be at work in the story of WCRC. Parmida spoke at length of how God had led her to WCRC. She said, "I felt God's hand, how should I say it, vividly in the way he led us to Willowdale." It is important to point out that, though the focus of this book is the human experience of welcome, many of the informants pointed out to God's leading in bringing them to WCRC and helping them to find a church home there. God at work was referenced twenty-eight times overall. Nikoo described receiving a US visa as a work of God because it was so hard for an Iranian family to receive one. Later, she also felt God leading her to WCRC, and she did not visit any other churches. Once at WCRC, she said she felt "God's presence." It is evident that the Holy Spirit has been at work at WCRC, in the members' openness, humility, and understanding.

---

32. Captari et al., "Prejudicial and Welcoming Attitudes," 135.

Discussion of Data

REFLEXIVITY

Wolcott notes that the main goal of the ethnographer is to "present the native's point of view as understood and relayed by the ethnographer."[33] The emic ethnography—or insider's view—is really about the ethnographer's version of the story of the group that is recounted.[34] In my case, I felt closer to the Farsi Fellowship members even though they felt more culturally distant. I think this is because I have been teaching once per month at the Farsi Fellowship for almost a year at the time of the research phase. As well, the Farsi Fellowship made extra time available to go over the project and prepare the members for the research phase. I was able to recruit Farsi-speaking Iranians quickly due to the efforts of the Farsi Fellowship leaders Adel and Parmida to introduce and explain the project. In contrast, the Sunday service did not allow a lot of time for introducing the project and answering questions and was limited to brief announcements by an elder before the congregational prayer. This meant that the project was given less of an introduction to the English speakers. To further complicate the situation, many of the English speakers attended church online even after in person services were permitted. That made it difficult to get to know the English-speaking members of the congregation. I missed them in the services I attended in person and when I had to attend my last service online due to bad weather, I was able to see many of the English speakers again on Zoom. This has led me to reflect that I had a closer relationship with the Farsi members during the research phase despite their being culturally more distant and so I may have been more attentive to their voice.

Conversely, during the interview phase, I found it easier to develop rapport with the English speakers, both in terms of language and culture. I found it harder to elicit responses from the Farsi-speaking Iranians, and their answers were usually shorter and more direct with less details and descriptions added. I was not sure if this was a language problem or a cultural phenomenon. It may be more about language because, when I interviewed Yara through a translator, his responses were longer and more descriptive as the interview series progressed,

---

33. Wolcott, *Ethnography*, 145.
34. Wolcott, *Ethnography*, 148.

and we had become more comfortable with the process. The challenge for me in interviewing Yara was that I found myself developing a rapport with Yara through with the translator. To sum up my feelings, I felt more familiar and comfortable with the Farsi-speaking community but more connected to the English-speaking community linguistically and culturally.

During the participant observation phase, I realized my presence in the Farsi Fellowship was causing some tension over the amount of translation that was happening. The Farsi Fellowship is an important opportunity for the community to come together and to speak Farsi. We resolved this issue by using WhatsApp for translation purposes while the meeting was going on and this seemed to work well.

I also experienced one meeting where there was a lot of conflict over an issue of interpretation of some Genesis passages. One member of the Farsi Fellowship brought an allegorical interpretation to the text, and this was opposed by Adel who preferred a more literal interpretation. Adel explained to me that people from an Islamic background needed a more literal and historical approach to the Bible as they had been raised to believe the Bible was all allegory, stories, and myths. I was not comfortable with this conflict and was unsure how much was cultural and how much was due to individual personalities. As the researcher, I was careful not to become involved. This was a new experience for me to experience this kind of conflict in this culture. I was told that this kind of conflict was, in fact, rare in the Farsi fellowship. Two Sundays later, the persons involved in the conflict showed a united front in the worship service. I highlight this to show that, even in such a tight knit community which is described in this research as a family, there can be conflict. This does not contradict the findings and perhaps even reinforces them.

SUMMARY

The data resulting from interviews with nine informants and participant observation of two weekly church events over a period of approximately two and a half months points to embodied practices of hospitality in welcoming and including a community of Farsi-speaking Iranians into an established Christian Reformed church in Toronto.

Discussion of Data

Certain themes stood out clearly among the informants and were, in some cases, also evident through participant observation. Some of the themes identified are the importance of a small group of both English- and Farsi-speaking church leaders who are committed to welcoming the stranger and working together toward a vision of a unified church. The sacraments were also important in welcoming Farsi-speaking newcomers, as were efforts to include elements of the Farsi language in the Sunday service, along with a dedicated Farsi-language meeting on Thursday evenings. The servant-leadership approach and efforts to involve newcomers quickly in social and volunteer activities was also key factor in both welcome and longer-term inclusion in the church of the Farsi-speaking Iranians. Including Farsi-speaking Iranians in ordained leadership in the church, too, was an important factor in inclusion. Sacramental hospitality played a very important role in the welcome of Farsi-speaking Iranians. The efforts at hospitality at WCRC was not without its challenges—particularly cultural differences and language barriers. In general, informants spoke of the warm welcome at WCRC. The study points to a general culture of welcome at WCRC that adapted well to the challenge and opportunity of Iranian newcomers coming to the church. The next chapter delves deeper into a theological reflection of the experience of welcome and inclusion at WCRC.

Chapter 5

Theological Reflection

HAVING DISCUSSED THE DATA findings of the ethnographic study at WCRC, this chapter provides a theological reflection on the domains and sub-domains identified by the informants. My foundation will be the pastoral cycle. A congregation is a good context for theological reflection because, as Pete Ward notes, "Church life makes each one of us into wise, skilled and highly accomplished theologians."[1] We could challenge Ward that church life has the potential to make us theologians only if theological reflection is applied through a careful methodology to the embodied practices that are experienced by the congregation. It is here that principles of practical theology can be helpful to a congregation and in this case to the leaders at WCRC. Farley also sees this as theology in its primary form, "namely, the reflective wisdom in the believer."[2] The role of practical theology is to "reflect critically and theologically on situations and to provide insights and strategies that will enable the movement towards faithful change."[3] Swinton and Mowat point out the "unique, revelatory role of the Church as the hermeneutic of the gospel: that place where the nature and purpose of the gospel is interpreted, lived out and revealed in the character and practice of those who would call themselves the Church."[4] Ward points

1. Ward, *Introducing Practical Theology*, 14.
2. Farley, "Interpreting Situations," 9.
3. Swinton and Mowat, *Practical Theology*, 24.
4. Swinton and Mowat, *Practical Theology*, 24.

to the importance of "absorbed theology" and how we live out of the residue within us that has been shaped by life in the Christian community.[5] The residue that Ward writes of can be called a *habitus*, or "knowledge as habit."[6]

The purpose of this study is to reflect on practices of hospitality or the *habitus* functioning at WCRC in a culture of welcome discovered through an ethnographic methodology. The main research question is how this culture came about and how it is functioning at present in welcoming the Farsi-speaking Iranians and how the Farsi-speaking Iranians are in turn impacting this culture. The reflection begins with practice as an embodied theology of welcome, then moves on to the foundation of Scripture and theological thought, then back to practice. To relate embodied practices of welcome to the foundation of Scripture, I adopt a linear approach as the most straightforward method for making this connection. Pritchard and Ballard note that this is the most basic form of theological reflection "whereby the Christian asks what biblical material . . . seems particularly relevant to the situation under review."[7]

METHODOLOGY

Scripture will be an important component of my reflection, which is something that Helen Collins encourages.[8] Collins advocates for the primacy of Scripture in the process of theological reflection because such reflection is not neutral and "contain[s] theological and epistemological assumptions that particularly conflict with the theological assumptions of charismatic, evangelical Christians."[9] A focus on Scripture is helpful to a community like WCRC because "individuals and communities seek to embody and act out the story of God told in Jesus."[10] This is important in grounding the embodied practices of hospitality at WCRC in the biblical narrative. In their practical theology,

---

5. Ward, *Introducing Practical Theology*, 17.
6. Ward, *Introducing Practical Theology*, 17.
7. Ballard and Pritchard, *Practical Theology in Action*, 129.
8. Collins, *Reordering*, 25.
9. Collins, *Reordering*, 8.
10. Graham et al., *Theological Reflection Methods*, 114.

Mark Branson and Alan Roxburgh recommend a cycle that begins with the analysis of praxis in its cultural context and then applies Christian texts and practices to the experience in order to discern God's agency and to shape new praxis in an ongoing cycle.[11] Robert Schreiter, in referring to congregational studies, notes that "theology does not exist in the abstract; it is always rooted in a context."[12] He further notes that studying a congregation is never a neutral process because it is always "laden with values, orientations, and understandings that the observer has accumulated over the years."[13] The starting points of reflection are the practices and rituals observed through the interviews and participant observation of the congregation.

I will add to this a correlational approach to include my social psychology conversation partners of social contact theory and social identity theory. Paul Tillich developed correlational methodology to process questions posed by secular existence that could be answered by Christian theology.[14] This correlational method also helped him to make connections between psychology and religion.[15] Correlational methods of theological reflection will have utility in thinking of the relationship between social theories and embodied hospitality in the congregation. A contextual approach to reflection is the most useful approach in an ethnographic study focused on the merging of two cultures. The pastoral cycle is most helpful as a tool for the congregation to process this information and allow it to shape congregational life and their continued pursuit of being a multicultural and multilingual congregation.

Ballard and Pritchard describe the pastoral cycle as beginning with present experience—routine life interrupted by external events—in this case, the arrival of a group of Farsi-speaking newcomers. The second phase is exploration. The analysis emerges from the lived experience of those involved. The third phase is reflection, which engages both personal and communal beliefs of the community, discoveries,

---

11. Branson and Roxburgh, *Leadership*, 74.
12. Schreiter, "Theology in the Congregation," 26.
13. Schreiter, "Theology in the Congregation," 26.
14. Graham et al., *Theological Reflection Methods*, 167.
15. Graham et al., *Theological Reflection Methods*, 168.

and changes. The final phase is the action step—it arises from the whole process. The cycle does not stop at this point but continues with further analysis and reflection.[16]

To summarize, I use a linear applied approach to theological reflection with a focus on context, culture, and an embodied hospitality evident in *habitus*. The advantage of the linear method is that biblical material and other sources of Christian truth that are relevant to the situation under review guide the reflection as it interacts with the lived experience.[17] The advantage of this method is that it is clear and "rooted in hundreds of years of scriptural or ecclesial authority."[18] The disadvantage is that this method may "assume a too simple relationship between tradition and practice."[19] It also may ignore God's "continuing self-revelation in history" and that "he might be creatively at work in other disciplines."[20] For this reason, I have decided to include some correlational method in order to include thoughts related to social contact and identity theory. This involves "a critical conversation of the distinctive elements of the situation under review, the human science or other material that throws light on it, and the theology that bears most directly."[21]

ENGLISH- AND FARSI-SPEAKING CHURCH LEADERS

Early in the interview process, I noticed numerous references to specific English- and Farsi-speaking church leaders. These leaders had made welcoming newcomers a part of their lives in such a way that it was evident it had become a *habitus*. They gravitated toward newcomers and embodied a theology of hospitality through physical space, language, and attitude. Though they were like fish swimming in a larger ocean of welcome, they were particularly intentional about living lives of welcome.

---

16. Ballard and Pritchard, *Practical Theology in Action*, 85–86
17. Ballard and Pritchard, *Practical Theology in Action*, 129.
18. Ballard and Pritchard, *Practical Theology in Action*, 130.
19. Ballard and Pritchard, *Practical Theology in Action*, 130.
20. Ballard and Pritchard, *Practical Theology in Action*, 130.
21. Ballard and Pritchard, *Practical Theology in Action*, 131.

This small group of people who intentionally and consistently welcomed people were a reminder of Jesus' reference to finding a person of peace in the Luke 10 narrative, where Jesus sends out the seventy-two disciples. Jesus tells the disciples in Luke 10:5–6 (NRSV), "Whatever house you enter, first say, 'Peace to this house!' And if anyone is there who shares in peace, your peace will rest on that person; but if not, it will return to you." Jesus wanted the disciples to look for specific people who would welcome them as guests and provide for them. If they found such people, they were to remain there and not move around. Five English-speaking leaders were named by the informants as being very welcoming in their experience. A small number of people committed to welcoming newcomers at WCRC made a huge difference in this story of hospitality. They were people of peace because they were willing to go out of their way to welcome newcomers. They were able to empathize with the newcomers with limited English skills and who were at times overwhelmed with change. They were open to learning about their experience and culture. They wanted to utilize the newcomer's gifts and abilities. They encouraged the use of the Farsi language in the Sunday service. They invited the newcomers into their homes.

For these leaders, their welcoming attitude and practice had become a *habitus*. Branson and Roxburgh describe *habitus* as "taken for granted ways a group of people live in relationship to one another and their context."[22] They also point out that the originator of the term Pierre Bordieu preferred *habitus* to the word "culture."[23] While there is a *culture* of welcome at WCRC, the term *habitus* better describes the agency of these individuals who made hospitality a tendency, propensity, and inclination.[24] Pohl points out, "We make a habit of hospitality when we remember how much Jesus is present in the practice."[25] James K. A. Smith further defines *habitus* as "the complex of inclinations and dispositions that make us lean into the world with a habituated momentum in certain directions."[26] Such inclinations propel the actors

22. Branson and Roxburgh, *Leadership*, 168.
23. Branson and Roxburgh, *Leadership*, 169.
24. Branson and Roxburgh, *Leadership*, 169.
25. Pohl, *Making Room*, 173.
26. Smith, *Imagining the Kingdom*, 79.

into actions and practices "without thinking." [27] This was true of the leaders identified as living out an embodied practice of hospitality. Although rooted in their belief that the gospel called them to welcome the stranger, their actions reflected a habituated inclination towards hospitality. They were—and continue to be—practitioners who are doers, fundamentally "acting in and upon their world."[28] Garces-Foley makes an important observation about such leaders in a multicultural setting from the minority community. She calls them "boundary crossers." She writes, "If not for their strong desire to be in a multicultural setting, few of these boundary crossers would stay the course."[29] She adds that they "bring skills for negotiating the ambiguity and discomfort that arise in a multicultural setting."[30] This points to the important role that the Farsi-speaking leaders in general have played in navigating and sustaining this multicultural experience. Despite ambiguity and discomfort, they persevered to continue to welcome newcomers and, collaborating with the English-speaking leaders, they formed a community of welcoming leaders at WCRC. The actions of both English- and Farsi-speaking leaders point to the difference that a few leaders can make in a congregational setting as they embody Christian hospitality to the stranger and make it a *habitus* of intentional and persistent welcome in a multicultural context.

ONE UNIFIED CHURCH TOGETHER

The decision to be one unified church together stands in contrast to the many ethnic and linguistic minority congregations renting church buildings as separate cultural communities. This is true of two other congregations in the WCRC building, Russian and Korean congregations. There is also a group of Tagalog-speaking worshipers meeting on Saturday nights for worship. For the Iranian leaders, their decision to be one body of Christ with the WCRC English-speaking congregation was stepping away from the ordinary. The then-pastor Aaron asked the Iranian leaders if they wanted to form their own group, but they

27. Smith, *Imagining the Kingdom*, 80.
28. Smith, *Imagining the Kingdom*, 80.
29. Garces-Foley, "New Opportunities and New Values," 222.
30. Garces-Foley, "New Opportunities and New Values," 222.

declined; they chose to have a separate meeting that functioned more like a Bible study, but they still wanted to come together as one church on Sundays. This was an intentional decision on the part of Adel and Parmida. They had come to WCRC seeking pastoral care themselves and wanted to be a part of the church.

Deciding to be one church was a decision to live out the eschatological vision of Rev 21 and 22 where the nations appear in the New Jerusalem and the Tree of Life is there and the leaves of the tree are for the healing of the nations. Churches that exhibit a variety of ethnicities and cultures reflect this heavenly vision. Van Opstal sees the importance of culture and context in the local expression of worship. She writes, "Jesus is the Savior of all people; every culture has gifts, and he welcomes their treasure as ways to honor and glorify him."[31] Referring to Rev 21, she writes, "In the end the beloved community, which consists of people from every nation, tribe, people and language, worships God."[32] It is worth noting that meeting together as one church allowed WCRC to move beyond hospitality to the other stages that Van Opstal sees as important in forming a multicultural worshipping community—solidarity and mutuality. Needing each other and being led by each other are signs of mutuality, and such signs are beginning to become apparent in the WCRC experience, especially with participation by the Farsi-speaking Iranians in worship and on the church council. Deymaz comments that, in building a healthy multiethnic church, it is important to call diverse representatives to join the leadership team.[33] Empowering diverse leaders has been an important principle of welcome and inclusion that WCRC has pursued intentionally.

Meeting together as two ethnicities and languages in one church certainly parallels Paul's teaching that there is no Jew or Gentile in the church. The church is one body together. It became clear that all the informants valued this one church approach and were able to express how the different linguistic and ethnic communities were a gift to each other. In this way, they were able to exemplify Paul's words in 1 Cor 12:12–13 (NRSV): "For just as the body is one and has many members,

---

31. Van Opstal, *Next Worship*, 31.
32. Van Opstal, *Next Worship*, 31.
33. Deymaz, *Building a Healthy Multi-Ethnic Church*, 154.

and all the members of the body, though many, are one body, so it is with Christ. For in the one Spirit we were all baptized into the one body—Jews or Greeks, slaves or free—and we were all made to drink of one Spirit." Richard Hays notes that in Paul's time, this rhetorical device of comparing the human body to human societies would have been used to keep subordinates in their places and in order to not upset the social order.[34] Paul, however, uses it to argue for diversity and interdependence and to "urge more privileged members of the community to respect and value those members who appear to be their inferiors, both in social status and spiritual potency."[35] The situation at WCRC closely resembles this dynamic, with the long term English speakers having a higher social status in the church and Canadian society while the Iranians are mostly getting established in their new country and, in many cases, making refugee claims in order to stay in Canada. The Iranian newcomers have very little status in Canadian society and in the church. Many of the Farsi-speaking Iranians are new Christians and so lack power in the church. They lack knowledge of theology and practice but are enthusiastic in the desire to learn. To use Hays's term, they lack spiritual potency.

Bringing these two groups together into one church better reflects Paul's analogy of the one body and the one church than it would have if they had remained two separate congregations. It also allows for the different gifts of the body to become apparent. Paul emphasizes the unity of the Spirit and that all believers are plunged together into a new world of "Spirit experience."[36] To quote Yong, "The Spirit brings about a new community out of radical diversity even while ensuring that diversity is preserved."[37] This work of the Spirit is an important finding: remaining together allowed each community to share their gifts with the other. Paul's body analogy rightly points out that each believer has gifts that are unique and that members of God's church are

---

34. Hays, *First Corinthians*, 213.
35. Hays, *First Corinthians*, 231.
36. Hays, *First Corinthians*, 214.
37. Yong, *Hospitality and the Other*, 58.

interdependent.³⁸ The importance of gifting became evident at WCRC through the course of my research.

A Gift to Each Other

Heather, one of the informants, mentioned the potential gifts of the Farsi-speaking newcomers, which led to my research question: "How are the Farsi-speaking Iranians a gift to WCRC? How is WCRC a gift to the Farsi-speaking Iranians?" Henri Nouwen, in *Reaching Out*, writes that when "hostility is converted into hospitality then fearful strangers can become guests revealing to their hosts the promise they are carrying with them. Then, in fact, the distinctions between host and guest proves to be artificial and evaporates in the recognition of the newfound unity."³⁹ De Bethune notes that the etymology of the English words "guest" and "host" come from the Indo-European root *ghosti*, which can mean both hostility and hospitality.⁴⁰ This means that the guest can be both friend and enemy. De Bethune concludes that converting hostility to hospitality means giving honour to the stranger, while not assimilating them. This leads to respecting difference while also transcending it. Recognizing the gifts that the guest and host bring to each other is an important part of this process.

Nouwen references the travelers on the road to Emmaus who invited the stranger to stay with them for the night, who made himself known to them as the resurrected Jesus in the breaking of the bread.⁴¹ In fact, Pastor Aaron had shared an Emmaus Road vision with the congregation in the face of a period of decline in the congregation and had encouraged the congregation to be open to new things that God may be doing. Pastor Aaron was actively preparing the congregation to receive the stranger and other unknown future opportunities for hospitality through this Emmaus Road vision. Norma shared, "He [Pastor Aaron] felt that God had a plan for our church, and he equated it to the road to Emmaus."

---

38. Hays, *First Corinthians*, 215.
39. Nouwen, *Reaching Out*, 67.
40. de Bethune, *Interreligious Hospitality*, 118.
41. Nouwen, *Reaching Out*, 67.

Theological Reflection

Fred Craddock notes that in the Emmaus Road narrative in Luke 24, the eyes of the disciples are opened in the breaking of the bread, and they recognize the stranger as Christ.[42] This is an important aspect of table hospitality and welcome and will be included as part of the reflection on the sacrament of the Lord's Supper at WCRC. Bock comments that the main purpose of this passage is to reassure us that Jesus is risen and alive.[43] Bock notes that the practical implication is that we do not need to be afraid that sin or the devil are more powerful than we are, but that we have Jesus' resurrection power to overcome "whatever obstacles Satan places in our past."[44] Jesus is alive, and he is present with the believer and the community of believers. One of the gifts that WCRC has given to the Farsi believers is weekly Lord's Supper where the rituals of Jesus' covenant renewal are acted out in a non-verbal way. Although the vision for weekly Lord's Supper preceded the first Iranian newcomers, their presence reinforced the importance of having the sacrament on every Sunday. The visual qualities of the Lord's Supper are helpful to those learning a new language because the weekly repetition brings comfort and understanding.

Nouwen gives other biblical examples of the gifts of the stranger. First, he writes of the visit by the three angelic visitors in Gen 18:1–15 and their announcement of a son for Sarah and Abraham. Another example is that, having received food and shelter from the widow of Zarephath, the prophet Elijah gives her an abundance of oil and meal and even raises her son from the dead, after she had offered him food and shelter (1 Kgs 17:9–24).[45] The gift of the stranger is an important biblical principle lived out in the WCRC context. Hebrews 13:2 encourages hospitality because "for by doing that some have entertained angels without knowing it" (NRSV). Pohl notes that the writer of Hebrews gives the account of the strangers' visit to Abraham and Sarah in Gen 18 a special status by referring to it in Heb 13:2. This is because the story of Abraham and the three visitors has a "persistent and formative

---

42. Craddock, *Luke*, 285.
43. Bock, *Luke*, 617.
44. Bock, *Luke*, 617.
45. Nouwen, *Reaching Out*, 66.

role in the instruction and motivation of the people of God.[46] Kim Sun, in formulating a Mennonite perspective on hospitality, includes in his list a mutual and joyful sharing of "God's abundant gifts that God has given both to the hosts and the guests."[47] Churches benefit when they give more attention to such opportunities for gift sharing in multicultural contexts.

Farsi-Speaking Iranians as a Gift to WCRC

The Farsi-speaking Iranians brought church renewal, inspiration, and energy. Pohl writes that, in most of the biblical stories related to hospitality, "guests brought their hosts into a special connection with God."[48] The Farsi-speaking Iranians brought new hope and life to WCRC in the context of an aging and declining congregation. The church found renewal and inspiration in welcoming the Iranian newcomers. Pohl notes that, in the important story of Abraham's hospitality to the three visitors, there is wonderful blessing.[49] This was evident in the interviews—though the Iranian newcomers brought challenges, they also brought great blessings.

One of the blessings that the Farsi-speaking Iranians brought to the church was baptism; over one-hundred-and-twenty baptisms were recorded. This large number of adult baptisms encouraged a congregation that had seen only a few infant baptisms a year. Written testimonies telling the stories of the candidates encouraged the congregation, some of which described persecution for the Christian faith in their home country. Although baptisms were performed in separate services due to COVID-19 restrictions, there was still a hopeful effect on the congregation. Heather, in one interview, pointed out that the large number of adult baptisms meant there was a large community in the church who could remember their baptisms and find spiritual strength and community in them.

Another blessing that came with the Farsi-speaking Iranians was a large population of children. This has been especially helpful for an

46. Pohl, *Making Room*, 24.
47. Kim Sun, "Mennonite Perspective," 298.
48. Pohl, *Making Room*, 26.
49. Pohl, *Making Room*, 26.

Theological Reflection

aging congregation and meant that Sunday School and youth programs could be revived. Despite the hindrance of COVID-19 restrictions, there were plans to restart Sunday school for children as soon as possible.

Farsi-speaking Iranians also brought musical gifts, and such gifts were used in worship. This was because Adel—as the Farsi-speaking leader—was quick to find volunteer opportunities for the Iranian newcomers and connected people to places where they could use their gifts. The music director did not hesitate to involve people in music, either, in Farsi or in English, in the public reading of Scripture, and in other ways of participating in the worship service. Van Opstal notes, "Global and ethnic partnerships across churches allow us to create spaces to engage in ethnically diverse worship. Sadly, this is seldom done."[50] WCRC has been able to create ethnically diverse worship. This was evident to me when I attended the worship service and listened to songs and prayers in Farsi. Van Opstal points to Rev 21 and its picture of all the nations bringing their glory and honour into the city. The church that involves itself in ethnically diverse worship looks ahead to the New Jerusalem.[51]

The opportunity to see the Christian faith through new eyes and to listen to a community that has been persecuted for their faith, too, was a gift. Informants expressed this as gratitude for the freedom of religion experienced in Canada which is sometimes taken for granted by the general population. Such gratitude is always positive when it is expressed in the context of a congregation. Paul notes in 1 Thess 5:18 that we are to give thanks in all circumstances. The Farsi-speaking Iranians brought this gift of gratitude to the church.

WCRC as a Gift to the Farsi-Speaking Iranians

WCRC brought safety and security, refugee hearing support, role models, family, and a context to learn Canadian culture and the English language. Pohl notes that "in ancient times hospitality included protection of the guest, and, when extended by a particular household, the entire community was bound to protect the guest."[52] Pohl writes, "Acts

---

50. Van Opstal, *Next Worship*, 51.
51. Van Opstal, *Next Worship*, 31.
52. Pohl, *Making Room*, 25.

of hospitality or inhospitality in the biblical narratives tended to reveal and reflect underlying good or evil of the person or community."[53] WCRC's provision of hospitality to the Farsi-speaking Iranians is evidence of a culture of hospitality that has existed for a long time. Refugee support has a long history as part of the Christian tradition of hospitality. Pohl notes that tying particular commitments and belief to material support is very dangerous. People need connection to living communities.[54] WCRC leaders chose to baptize all who came once they had expressed a desire to follow Jesus and be a part of the church. This was also true for Peter von Kaehne's community in the UK. They decided to baptize without delving into internal motivations.[55] The advantage of this, as Pohl observes, is that "it allows for a constant, complex interaction between identity-defining, bounded communities and a larger community with minimal boundaries that offers basic protections of individuals."[56]

While safety and security are extremely important, Farsi-speaking Iranians are also looking for a family—in this case, the family of God. Many of the newcomers have left family behind. Some informants have family in Canada, but this was not as common as leaving family behind, and this was felt during important holidays such as the Iranian New Year celebration or *Nowruz*. Farsi-speaking Iranians found family first in the Farsi Fellowship and then in the larger church family in WCRC. Paul in his salutation to the Galatians in Gal 1:2 refers to "all the members of God's family who are with me." God's family was evident in WCRC.

Farsi-speaking Iranians mentioned the gift of English-speaking older members of the congregation as role models of the Christian faith. The Farsi-speaking Iranians—many of whom are new believers—spoke of the importance of having guides to Christian life and practice. Paul models this in 2 Tim 1:13–14: "Whatever you heard from me, keep as the pattern of sound teaching, with faith and love in Christ Jesus. Guard the good deposit that was entrusted to you— guard it with

---

53. Pohl, *Making Room*, 26.
54. Pohl, *Making Room*, 83.
55. von Kaehne, "Iranian Diaspora Ministry," 445.
56. Pohl, *Making Room*, 83.

Theological Reflection

the help of the Holy Spirit who lives in us" (NIV). Little notes that the New Testament picture of spiritual growth "envisions people growing by living together in Spirit-led and Spirit-graced communities."[57] The English-speaking members could help the Iranian newcomers learn about Canadian culture and practice English. As Edward noted in an interview, the church is an opportunity to learn about all things Canadian including Tim Horton's coffee or skating. As noted by the informants, the sacraments served as a gift that Willowdale offered to the Farsi-speaking Iranians. On a deeper level, both English- and Farsi-speaking members became guests of God's sacramental hospitality through baptism and the Lord's Supper leading to a beautiful mutuality.

THE SACRAMENTS

Sacramental hospitality is an important component of the congregational welcome at WCRC. This is because baptism is a rite of initiation in the Christian church. Eucharistic hospitality of the Lord's Supper played an important role in the life of the church as highlighted by the informants. Both sacraments reflected an important theological language of inclusion and hospitality. In the Reformed tradition of both the Lord's Supper and baptism, God is the initiator and the host, and all who participate are guests. This moves the guest-versus-host or us-versus-them dynamic towards mutuality. It is important to note that the sacraments reinforced other domains in the research. For example, the sacrament of baptism contributed to the idea of being one unified church together and gave those baptized a new identity, which was important in forming a new superordinate identity and is also important in social identity theory of group cohesion. Baptism also reinforced the idea of being family together and belonging to the church. The sacrament of the Lord's Supper reminded the participants of God's promises and allowed the Farsi newcomers to participate in a ritual that transcended both language and culture and nurtured their nascent faith.

In the sacraments, God welcomes all people. In the case of the Lord's Supper, there is no in-group or out-group. All people are welcomed to the table by God who is the host. Bavinck notes that Luther,

---

57. Little, *Effective Discipling*, 134.

Zwingli, and Calvin "taught that the sacraments imparted forgiving grace, that it was valueless without the Word, and its operation presupposed faith in the recipient."[58] Calvin further taught that the sacraments of the Lord's Supper and baptism were signs and seals of God's promises in the covenant of grace.[59] The sacraments serve to help the believer to understand God's promises, be reassured of them, and receive the benefits of God's covenant of grace.[60]

Reformed theology "describes the sacraments as visible, holy signs and seals instituted by God."[61] Bavinck observes that on this point there is no disagreement in the Christian churches. As God institutes the sacraments, God is then host of the sacrament, and the believer is the guest at the table. This unifies the church as recipients of God's grace as all are equally sinners who are in need of God's grace. This puts everyone in the same place and takes away any kind of us-versus-them dynamic in the church between host and guest, long-time members and newcomers, or between residents and refugees. Paul expounds on this line of thought of all being welcome to the table in the context of the Corinthian church in 1 Cor 11. Paul is arguing for a beautiful mutuality of one body of Christ together as guests all hosted by God. This hospitality was embodied in the decision of WCRC to hold the Lord's Supper weekly and by freely baptizing all newcomers who made a profession of faith and desired to become part of the church.

Baptism

As Heather stated, "There are many people now at Willowdale who remember their baptism." This brings new vitality to WCRC with regular baptisms in the Farsi-speaking community. Heather stated that there were over one-hundred baptisms in the last two years, most of which were adult baptisms. Before the Iranian newcomers came to WCRC, there were very few baptisms. Most Christian Reformed congregations perform a few infant baptisms per year, so WCRC is unique in having so many adult baptisms. Sophie also commented that, in baptism,

58. Bavinck, *Reformed Dogmatics*, 461.
59. Bavinck, *Reformed Dogmatics*, 462.
60. Bavinck, *Reformed Dogmatics*, 462.
61. Bavinck, *Reformed Dogmatics*, 473.

Theological Reflection

God is the active host and that God's mission is evident as the church welcomes new believers to be baptized and become members. In conjunction with baptism services, the leaders of the Farsi Fellowship published testimonies of baptism candidates. These testimonies were distributed to members of the congregation to read. Through these stories, the congregation experienced the faith journeys and struggles of the Iranian newcomers. These stories encouraged the believers and unified the congregation. They also played an important role in communication during the pandemic, during which only small groups could gather for baptism services. The services were in both Farsi and English with translation. The identities of the candidates for baptism were protected—often using first names only and with warnings not to distribute the stories or post them on the Internet—to provide safety and security to the Iranian candidates.

Baptism is a historically and theologically significant rite of initiation into the Christian church.[62] Bavinck notes that believers entered the church through baptism in the apostolic era.[63] Sacramental thinking developed further during medieval scholasticism leading up to seven sacraments. J. D. C. Fisher looks at the historical development of the initiatory rite and its development from the seventh century onward into three separate rites: baptism, confirmation, and first communion in the church in the West.[64] During the Reformation, the Reformers limited the sacraments to two: baptism and the Lord's Supper. In the Reformed tradition, a profession of faith usually precedes the baptism of an adult. In the case of infant baptism, the parents of the child profess their faith. Communion is not mandatory after the baptism of adults or infants. Calvin understood the sacraments as distributed by God and as signs and seals of God's covenantal grace.[65] Bavinck notes that baptism must be connected to the faith of the individual and to the word of God. He

---

62. For further reading on the biblical and historical development of baptism as a rite of initiation, see Porter and Cross, eds., *Baptism, the New Testament and the Church*; Wainwright, *Christian Initiation*; Beasley-Murray, *Baptism in the New Testament*; Riley, *Christian Initiation*.

63. Bavinck, *Reformed Dogmatics*, 461.

64. Fisher, *Christian Initiation*, xi.

65. Bavinck, *Reformed Dogmatics*, 463.

writes that, if baptism is disconnected, "it is robbed of its scriptural character and ceases to be a sign and seal of God's promises."[66]

Leonard Vander Zee points out an important theological distinction in the Reformed understanding of baptism, which is that "the central action of baptism belongs to God."[67] He argues that both Luther and Calvin believed that, in the sacraments, God acted through visible signs and seals. This was in opposition to Zwingli who believed the sacraments were expressions of human faith in God's actions through Christ. Vander Zee writes, "For Calvin and Luther, baptism is about what God is doing and promising to us."[68] This is important in our understanding of sacramental hospitality—both in baptism and in the Lord's Supper—God is host, and all who participate are guests. This is God's gracious welcome into the church for all people—in case of WCRC, for both English speakers and Farsi-speaking Iranians.

Baptism was one of the gifts that WCRC could give to the Farsi-speaking Iranians, and it was offered only as a gracious vehicle of God's welcome and grace. Baptism strengthened the unity of the church and reinforced the one unified church idea. Paul writes in Eph 4:4–6, "There is one body and one Spirit, just as you were called to the one hope of your calling, one Lord, one faith, one baptism, one God and Father of all, who is above all, and through all, and in all" (NRSV). Michael Green sees the theme of unity in this passage. He writes that there are seven references to "one" that spring from the unity of God.[69] All Farsi informants mentioned the importance of their baptism as a step of faith and a milestone on their spiritual journey. Green sees baptism as representing three important aspects of the Christian life: Those who are baptized enter into the family of God; they accept God's offer of love and surrender their lives to him; and they are filled with the Holy Spirit.[70] As Heather mentioned, the Farsi-speaking Iranians remember their baptisms and retain those memories, which gives them strength

---

66. Bavinck, *Reformed Dogmatics*, 498.
67. Vander Zee, *Christ, Baptism and the Lord's Supper*, 102.
68. Vander Zee, *Christ, Baptism and the Lord's Supper*, 103.
69. Green, *Baptism*, 12.
70. Green, *Baptism*, 20.

Theological Reflection

in difficult times. Baptism has been an important way of welcoming the newcomer at WCRC.

An important practice of this welcome is not questioning motives for those requesting baptism. In doing this, WCRC is following an understanding of baptism that is biblical. Vander Zee observes that there is no way of knowing that all members of the visible church are true believers. Quoting Matt 13:30, he writes, "Wheat and the tares grow together until the harvest in the church as well as in the world."[71] He concludes that it is up to God to make this judgment.[72] A profession of faith is always required before baptism, and this occurs at WCRC. But as Louis Berhof writes, "It does not belong to her providence to pry into the secrets of the heart and thus to pass on the genuineness of such a profession. The responsibility rests on the person who makes it."[73]

In the practice of the sacrament, baptism represents the washing away of the pollution of sin, just as water washes away dirt. Baptism is a sign of the regeneration that comes through Christ and the faith of the individual, in which the water serves as a visible sign and seal of that reality.[74] Bavinck notes that the water of baptism becomes a sacrament through the words of institution. WCRC is faithful to this requirement through the baptismal liturgy. An interpreter translates different parts of the baptismal service into Farsi. Robert Browning and Roy Reed note the importance and power of the symbols, which is to address "the deeper spiritual hunger present in the lives of people."[75] This was true for the Farsi-speaking informants who spoke of the importance of the sacraments. Smith writes that, in many ways, "baptism is a microcosm of the entirety of Christian worship and the story of God, in Christ, reconciling the world to himself."[76] The separation of baptism services from the main worship service is a challenge for WCRC, and it will be imperative for the leadership to re-integrate baptism services into the main congregational worship as the pandemic allows.

---

71. Vander Zee, *Christ, Baptism and the Lord's Supper*, 113.
72. Vander Zee, *Christ, Baptism and the Lord's Supper*, 113.
73. Berkhof, *Systematic Theology*, 632.
74. Bavinck, *Reformed Dogmatics*, 497.
75. Browning and Reed, *Sacraments*, 76.
76. Smith, *Desiring the Kingdom*, 182.

An important correlation is that baptism is a sacrament of identity. Vander Zee notes that baptism is an identifier of a new identity in Christ, that is, "a new humanity set free from sin and death."[77] This is why new believers are baptized into the name of Jesus. In baptism, believers are given a new identity.[78] According to Tory Baucum, conversion is the "transformation of identity concurrent with a new primary reference group and its worldview."[79] Conversion can be understood psycho-socially as an alteration of one's identity. When identity transformation happens in a group, it is called "encapsulation." Baucum outlines five components of the self that undergo reconstruction in the process: attitudes, values, behaviours, roles, and self-concept. [80]

This new identity becomes a communal or superordinate identity that unites the group and gives cohesion, especially when two very different cultural groups come together to form one community. Baptism allows the in-group and the out-group both to express their identity individually and to begin to form a superordinate identity. For example, in the case of Farsi-speaking Iranians coming for baptism, an important part is to be able to tell their story of how they came to faith and the trials and triumphs involved in such a narrative. At WCRC, these stories were made available to other members of the congregation. COVID-19 limitations meant that these stories could not be shared verbally, but they were distributed in print form. This is important for the identity within the group. However, for long-term cohesion, the superordinate identity has to take precedence. This can only happen when the salience of the new identity grows greater than the old identity. Baptism—and especially a baptism that is significant and memorable—is part of this transition. Baptism leads to a superordinate identity of being God's child and a member of God's church. Baptism is a memorable and meaningful initiation into the Christian faith and into the church. Identity is fluid and fluctuates, but baptism does serve as a means of grace to this new identity. Baptism at WCRC

---

77. Vander Zee, *Christ, Baptism and the Lord's Supper*, 109.
78. Smith, *Desiring the Kingdom*, 191.
79. Baucum, *Evangelical Hospitality*, 21.
80. Baucum, *Evangelical Hospitality*, 28.

serves to reinforce God's gracious welcome to the Iranian newcomers through this sacrament.

Volf notes the importance of allegiance "only to the God of 'all the families on earth,' not to any particular county, culture, or family with their local deities."[81] This is an important function of baptism as orientation to a new family and identity that supersedes old categories or group identification. This is important especially in situations where groups may be in conflict. Volf also highlights a transformation at the heart of Christian identity, affirmed in baptism, as an "all-encompassing change of loyalty, from a given culture with its gods to the God of all cultures."[82] In baptism, the old gods must now submit to the God of all culture, ethnicity, and family.

Finally, baptism has an important role in the mission of the church. Geoffrey Wainwright points out the link between Christian initiation and mission. He writes, "Baptism both introduces one into the community which knows the benefits of salvation and also imposes on one the obligation of participating in the further prosecution of the saving mission."[83] Frederick Brunner ties together Jesus' baptism at the beginning of the Gospel of Matthew with the command to go and baptize at the end of the Gospel. Bruner sees the practical purpose of Jesus' baptism as "ministry opening," that is, "to teach the church what happens to her in these events: a great deal."[84] The role of baptism in WCRC is not only about membership and renewal in the church but also about the mission of God to Farsi-speaking Iranians and all people who encounter God's grace through the people of WCRC.

Lord's Supper

Pastor Aaron's Emmaus Road vision convinced the leaders of WCRC to decide to hold the Lord's Supper every Sunday.[85] Calvin wanted to hold

---

81. Volf, *Exclusion and Embrace*, 39.
82. Volf, *Exclusion and Embrace*, 40.
83. Wainwright, *Christian Initiation*, 71.
84. Bruner, *Matthew*, 109.
85. For a biblical and historical overview of the sacrament of the Lord's Supper, see Thurian and Wainwright, eds., *Baptism and Eucharist*; McGowan, *Ancient Christian Worship*; Boersma and Levering, eds., *The Oxford Handbook of Sacramental*

the Lord's Supper weekly in Geneva to reflect the apostolic period, but the city council did not agree with his recommendation and decided to hold it four times a year, a common practice in Christian Reformed churches today.[86] Claudio Carvalhaes notes that Calvin's innovation in the Lord's Supper was to move the locus of power from the church to the Holy Spirit in the individual believer. This meant that that the focus was on the transcendent God and not on the human institution.[87] This reminds us that God is the host of the Lord's Supper, not the church or the leaders of the church. This is important in confronting the us-versus-them dynamic between the groups in the church. All are guests at the table of God, and this encourages mutuality.

In teaching of the real spiritual presence of Christ in the elements, as opposed to the actual physical manifestation as taught in the Roman Catholic Church at the time, Carvalhaes writes, "We can say that God moves freely and unconstrainedly around the table."[88] This means that Christ's Incarnation is not limited by any material manifestations but "opens itself to endless possibilities of expression and experience in multiple cultural manifestations/spaces."[89] This means that the Holy Spirit can work through the sacrament in and through different cultures and languages, encouraging God's work in the heart of the believers, whether a new Canadian from Iran or an older member of the congregation with a Dutch background.

One of the gifts of the Reformation was the focus on God's presence in the sacrament. Thus, "God's presence, sacramentally experienced, was not a product of human effort or ritual action."[90] The idea of the real presence of Jesus in the sacrament meant that the "Holy Spirit was at work, using the elements, word, gesture, and the faith of believers to effect an intimate encounter with the reality of Christ."[91] Calvin's approach recognized that the Holy Spirit was feeding and nurturing

---

Theology; Ferguson, ed., *Studies in Early Christianity*.

86. Carvalhaes, *Eucharist and Globalization*, 84.
87. Carvalhaes, *Eucharist and Globalization*, 90.
88. Carvalhaes, *Eucharist and Globalization*, 95.
89. Carvalhaes, *Eucharist and Globalization*, 95.
90. Carvalhaes, *Eucharist and Globalization*, 101.
91. Carvalhaes, *Eucharist and Globalization*, 102.

Theological Reflection

the spiritual growth of the congregation on a weekly basis. This process effected by the Holy Spirit "was why Calvin insisted on the importance of frequent attendance at worship and sought to have Eucharist celebrated at least once a week."[92] Carvalhaes does note the importance of words in the Eucharistic ritual.[93] This is because for Christ the Word is central to the sacrament. This does point to the importance of including the Apostles' Creed in Farsi in preparation for the Lord's Supper at WCRC. It also raises the question as to whether more translation should happen in the preparatory elements of the Lord's Supper. The ritual is familiar and meaningful but needs the word to complete the experience of faith and understanding God's grace for salvation. On the other hand, the ritual can also be called a "locus of revelation."

Carvalhaes points out the mystical side of Calvin's view of the limits of understanding God and the need to experience God in the Eucharist.[94] Despite the limits of human sinfulness and the predilection to create idols that Calvin was so concerned about regarding icons, the Lord's Supper does involve our bodies, our physical movements, and senses, and thus becomes a "locus of God's revelation."[95] This opens up possibilities for a Reformed embodied theology of hospitality that seems to be taking place at WCRC. Despite limitations and concerns of the danger of overemphasizing human ritual, God does communicate in these ways, and "God's accommodation is, in many ways, an embodied accommodation."[96] Carvalhaes points out that God's freedom to be and manifest himself anywhere leads to many possibilities of ritual embodiment in the Lord's Supper.[97] This is a helpful perspective for Farsi-speaking newcomers participating in the Lord's Supper which transcends language and culture in order to nurture faith on a weekly basis.

This ritual embodiment points to the important principle of Eucharistic hospitality: God hosts all members of WCRC in the Eucharist.

---

92. Carvalhaes, *Eucharist and Globalization*, 104.
93. Carvalhaes, *Eucharist and Globalization*, 105.
94. Carvalhaes, *Eucharist and Globalization*, 115.
95. Carvalhaes, *Eucharist and Globalization*, 116.
96. Carvalhaes, *Eucharist and Globalization*, 116.
97. Carvalhaes, *Eucharist and Globalization*, 117.

As L. Gregory Jones points out, experiencing the Lord's Supper is an eschatological act that looks forward to the communion of saints. The Lord's Supper is a trans-historical and international practice that reminds us that, wherever we come from, we are united as Christians around the table.[98] Eucharistic hospitality is a way for the dominance of the host and the suspicion of the guest to be overcome as all participate in the way of Jesus that brings outsiders in.[99] Jones notes that Jesus' table fellowship is all about bringing in the marginalized and outcasts, sinners and tax collectors into his presence, changing the parameters of the community.[100] Eucharistic hospitality also helps to avoid some of the paternalism that can develop when a church invites a group of people in need. We not only want our guests to survive but also want them to flourish by becoming part of our lives *as honoured guests*. It also recognizes that we are all sinners and alienated from God, but that God welcomes us in through Christ. All church members are transformed from strangers into friends and can pass the peace because Jesus is the Prince of Peace.[101]

One innovation at WCRC is that individuals who express interest in being at church, following the Christian religion, and committing their lives to Christ, are permitted to partake of the Lord's Supper. Eucharistic hospitality is symbolized by the open table. In the case of WCRC, the standard practice is to fence the Lord's Supper with a statement that the practice is for believers only. While this practice continues at WCRC, those who are not yet baptized have been allowed to participate in the Lord's Supper. This is a way of welcoming the stranger in the weekly practices of the church as opposed to excluding them from an important weekly ritual while they wait for baptism (e.g., in uncertain COVID-19 times). Browning and Reed argue that an eschatological interpretation that emphasizes the kingdom aspects of the Lord's Supper opens the table to all, even to the unbaptized.[102] The Lord's Supper looks ahead to the banquet in the new heaven and new

---

98. Jones, "Eucharistic Hospitality," 16.
99. Jones, "Eucharistic Hospitality," 16.
100. Jones, "Eucharistic Hospitality," 15.
101. Jones, "Eucharistic Hospitality," 16.
102. Browning and Reed, *Sacraments*, 172.

earth. They conclude by saying, "All guests from wherever they come are to be welcomed."[103] Further, "no one should be refused communion who has been moved by the celebration."[104] In the WCRC context, many newcomers participated in the Lord's Supper in their journey of discovering Christianity, even before they were baptized. Browning and Reed note that the Lord's Supper is part of the "life giving, joyous faith of the community."[105] Communion has a nurturing effect on believers and is an important part of their spiritual development.[106] In this way, WCRC expressed Eucharistic hospitality.

The Apostles' Creed is recited in English with a printed Farsi translation. This added an element of doctrinal teaching around the Lord's Supper. There is a tension in that the Farsi-speaking informants expressed appreciation for the nonverbal elements of the Lord's Supper, while the word of God remains central to the sacrament in Reformed doctrine. Preparing for the Lord's Supper through reciting the Apostles' Creed helps alleviate this tension. Smith points out the importance of such creedal statements in the baptismal liturgy, and this is applicable to the Lord's Supper as well. He writes, "The Apostles' Creed functions like the church's pledge of allegiance."[107] When recited weekly, it serves as a reminder of God's promises sealed in baptism, as well as functioning as a "citizenship-renewal ceremony" in which the citizens of the new *polis* (community) reaffirm their allegiance.[108] Reciting the Apostles' Creed ties the congregation into the larger Christian church—both current and historical. It constitutes the church as a people of memory.[109] This is important for all members of the church as it is again unifying. It is helpful for Farsi-speaking newcomers who come from a different historical, cultural, and religious tradition.

The Lord's Supper at WCRC has a unifying function. The sacrament reinforces the decision to be one unified church together both in

---

103. Browning and Reed, *Sacraments*, 172.
104. Browning and Reed, *Sacraments*, 172.
105. Browning and Reed, *Sacraments*, 172.
106. Browning and Reed, *Sacraments*, 172.
107. Smith, *Desiring the Kingdom*, 190.
108. Smith, *Desiring the Kingdom*, 191.
109. Smith, *Desiring the Kingdom*, 191.

worship and in the sacraments. There is no privileged place at WCRC, as there was at the Corinthian church. Pohl writes, "In the context of shared meals, the presence of God's kingdom is prefigured, revealed and reflected."[110] For Pohl, the Lord's Supper continually "reenacts the center of the gospel."[111] This is why it was so helpful that the leaders of WCRC decided to move to a weekly Lord's Supper as an act of hospitality even before the first Iranian newcomers arrived. Pohl also sees an eschatological purpose in the Lord's Supper, pointing to the "heavenly table of the Lord."[112]

Paul's experience with the Lord's Supper in the Corinthian church in 1 Cor 11 is helpful for reflecting on the power dynamics experienced during the Lord's Supper at WCRC. The problem that Paul was addressing related to some Corinthian Christians eating and drinking ahead of the others and indulging in better food and drink. Such practices reflected Roman society that put privileged patrons at the head table at banquets with better food and drink. While some of the privileged Corinthian Christians were eating and getting drunk on wine, other less advantaged Christians were going hungry in the feasts that were connected to the Lord's Supper. These practices brought disunity to the Corinthian church. Richard Hays notes that the Greek word συνέρχομαι is repeated five times in this section, playing on the phrase "to come together" and revealing that the Corinthian Christians were not *coming together* in unity and peace.[113] At WCRC, the Lord's Supper has brought unity to the church and reinforced the concept of one unified church. This has happened due to the decision to celebrate the Lord's Supper weekly with a simple liturgy that is repeated from week to week. This has been advantageous for the Farsi newcomers who learn the rituals and become comfortable with the process that transcends language and becomes a unifying practice across language groups. It was noted that, before COVID-19, the Farsi-speaking newcomers were led down to the front to partake of communion.

---

110. Pohl, *Making Room*, 30.
111. Pohl, *Making Room*, 30.
112. Pohl, *Making Room*, 30.
113. Hays, *First Corinthians*, 194.

Theological Reflection

The Lord's Supper at WCRC continued despite COVID-19. Pohl points to the importance of shared meals. Informants highlighted times of eating together as significant events for them before the pandemic. These meals were important times of learning about the other culture. With the coming of the pandemic and related restrictions, these meals stopped. However, the Lord's Supper continued as an important ritualistic meal for the congregation and for the newcomers. Even though the sacrament was limited to small cups with wafers sealed inside, Diba referred to his experience of thinking about the taste of that small wafer throughout the day.

Pastor Aaron's vision of the Emmaus Road was a way for the congregation to be open to what God could do in welcoming the other. In the breaking of the bread, Cleopas and his companion have their eyes opened and realize that their guest is Jesus. Pastor Aaron sensed the Spirit's call to prepare the way, and though he may not have realized how important the weekly Lord's Supper would become in welcoming the Farsi-speaking Iranians at WCRC, his vision has come to a beautiful fruition.

CULTURE OF WELCOME

The embodied sacramental hospitality reflects the culture of welcome at WCRC. Informants who came to the church ten to fifteen years ago noted a general culture of welcome at WCRC, which was long before the first Iranian couple arrived. Pohl writes, "Hospitality is not optional for Christians, nor is it limited to those who are especially gifted for it."[114] The English-speaking informants mentioned key individuals who had been welcoming to them ten to fifteen years ago. The people of WCRC have put flesh on the gospel by welcoming the stranger into their church and their homes for a long time—they developed a *habitus* of welcome. So, when Adel and Parmida came, they were warmly welcomed, and in turn, Adel and Parmida could welcome other Farsi-speaking Iranians to WCRC through their global connections within the Persian community. Thus, a cycle of welcome developed leading to an expanding group of Farsi-speaking Iranians. This not only led

---

114. Pohl, *Making Room*, 31.

to a positive experience of welcome but also helped with the process of inclusion over the longer term for these Farsi-speaking newcomers.

Branson and Roxburgh explain in more detail what such a *habitus* looks like in a congregation: "It involves things like heritage and traditions, the normative ways of acting in a group, the feelings and emotions common to a group."[115] They further define *habitus* as consisting of embodied practices.[116] In a sense, practices are the ways in which a group goes about working out its *habitus*. This means that the culture of welcome at WCRC is evident in the practices of the members, especially of the leaders. This *habitus* of welcome has become extremely important in the life of the congregation in the face of decline and aging. This *habitus* allowed the congregation to welcome many newcomers over the last three years and to cope with much change and disruption. This is because a *habitus* is not part of any particular strategy (although it did seem to be initiated by Pastor Aaron's Emmaus Road vision for change). This *habitus* of welcome was used by God to bring change in a way that the congregation could manage in a time of disruption. The large number of newcomers from Iran challenges the church to continue to develop new practices of inclusion and a new *habitus* of mutuality as a congregation. Ammerman notes that new members change the culture of a congregation by bringing in new expectations, experiences, and connections, and therefore one would expect that they would also influence the *habitus* of a congregation.[117] It is important that church leaders are aware of and attuned to this *habitus*, and that they know how it is changing and shaped by the newcomers in the midst of change. This *habitus* can be observed in specific practices of the congregation.

PRACTICES OF WELCOME

Pohl observes, "One of the simplest ways of communicating welcome is to greet guests at the door or threshold and personally escort them in."[118] Over the years, this has become a *habitus* at WCRC. Informants like

---

115. Branson and Roxburgh, *Leadership*, 168.
116. Branson and Roxburgh, *Leadership*, 170.
117. Ammerman, "Cultural and Identity," 90.
118. Pohl, *Making Room*, 181.

Theological Reflection

Edward mentioned a greeter at the door who had been at the church for several years. Not only was the greeter mentioned but also the greeter's specific practices such as eye contact, physical handshakes, connecting people to other people, and home hospitality were mentioned. Pohl notes that "guests feel welcome when someone orients them to a new place. This may involve helping them through an unfamiliar liturgy or showing them the coffee pot."[119] It was mentioned that pre-COVID, Adel would often go to the front for communion with the newcomers from Iran to help them participate in an unfamiliar context. Another innovation was the post-sermon discussion that Pastor Aaron encouraged specifically for the Farsi-speaking Iranians to be able to ask questions and to grow in their faith.

According to Pohl, such practices are important for a congregation. She writes, "We must intentionally nurture a commitment to hospitality. It must be nurtured because the blessings and the benefits are not always immediately apparent."[120] She also says, "We nurture hospitality as a habit and a disposition by telling stories about it."[121] In some ways, that is the purpose of this book—that is, to tell those stories of hospitality at WCRC. Many of the informants, both English- and Farsi-speaking Iranians, had little difficulty in sharing a story of hospitality, both given and received. Pohl encourages hospitality to become a *habitus* in the congregation. This was observed as a generational phenomenon, part of the culture of WCRC, presently lived out by seven key leaders who are very welcoming. Pohl comments that one of the challenges today for churches practicing hospitality is the busyness of life. I observed through interviews that busyness was a challenge for the Farsi-speaking Iranians, especially for new Canadians with many demands on their time, but not so much for the English speakers, many of whom are older adults and retired. This allowed them to have more time to practice hospitality.

Another important practice observed at WCRC is recognition of the other, the stranger, the newcomer, and affirmation of their human personhood. Pohl writes, "Simple acts of respect and appreciation,

---

119. Pohl, *Making Room*, 181.
120. Pohl, *Making Room*, 171.
121. Pohl, *Making Room*, 173.

presence and friendship are indispensable parts of the affirmation of human personhood."[122] Recognition is an important practice of welcome. It also leads to further welcome and inclusion. Pohl notes, "Hospitality offers a model for developing reciprocal relationships."[123] Such relationships are important for changing from an us-versus-them mentality and dynamic in the church to a mutuality that respects differences but works towards togetherness, service, and recognition.

Friendship, as seen in a growing community of friends, increases unity, mutuality, social cohesion, and congregational health. I noted in interviews that friendships between English-speaking and Farsi-speaking members of the church were forming. Norma, for example, spoke of working with a new Farsi-speaking deacon on financial matters. Shadan mentioned the importance of friendships in the church ("just normal friendships"). Parmida also mentioned that friendship building was an important part of Adel's ministry, which involved speaking on the phone, hearing their stories, and being a friend. Such friendships are part of a longer-term relationship of welcome that are a critical part of the journey of hospitality. Brother John of Taizé writes of friendship from a biblical perspective, mainly drawing from John 15. Jesus calls believers his "friends," and then church members develop friendships with others in this spirit. Jesus' friendship is about being servant hearted, putting the other first, and growing in love. Brother John writes that when friendship excludes anyone from outside, it becomes about human affability and is superficial and less inclusive, but when it is rooted in Christ, it becomes open to friendship with the person who is different.[124] In John 15, Jesus calls his disciples "friends" because he has brought them close through his life, teaching, and ultimately his death on the cross. Jesus commands them to love one another, which is central to biblical friendship.[125] Brother John sees this as a critical movement for the church: He writes, "To foster the growth of a community of friends, that in turn, manifests a community on earth (always imperfectly, 'on the road,' as it were) the *koinonia* of the invisible

---

122. Pohl, *Making Room*, 84.
123. Pohl, *Making Room*, 162.
124. Brother John of Taizé, *Friends in Christ*, 133.
125. Brother John of Taizé, *Friends in Christ*, 89.

God."[126] This practice of friendship is an important part of hospitality at WCRC and towards their journey to mutuality.

EXPERIENCE OF WELCOME

Words such as "warm," "trust," "love," "peace," "comfort," and "kind" were used by informants to describe their experience of hospitality. These words point to the importance of reducing the anxiety that comes with entering a new place, a new and unfamiliar environment for the stranger. It also points to the importance of human contact and of connections to others that might have something in common, who can forge relationships, to lessen anxiety. Most of these references related to in-person visits to the church and were references to pre-pandemic times. Embodying the gospel of love should produce positive feelings. I noted that Farsi-speaking Iranians who had come during COVID-19 and had mainly experienced the church through Zoom meetings still expressed some of these feelings. Brother John of Taizé notes, "The only infallible proof that we are in communion with the mystery of God is the active love we show to those around us."[127] Such love is apparent in the comments made by the informants, and Parmida specifically said that their ministry strategy was to love, above all, the Farsi-speaking newcomers. She added, "What we strive to do by God's grace is to share the love, just be friendly, be friends with them, listen to them, and try to embrace even their challenges." This approach was born out in the comments made about the experience of welcome focusing on warmth, trust, love, peace, comfort, and kindness.

GUEST-HOST DYNAMICS

Guest–host dynamics are important in the WCRC context because there are a large number of Farsi-speaking Iranians who are guests joining an established church who is host. This creates a perceived power differential between host and guest. During the writing of this book, I applied to present at the BIAPT (British & Irish Association for Practical Theology; www.biapt.org) conference. The convener's

---

126. Brother John of Taizé, *Friends in Christ*, 122.
127. Brother John of Taizé, *Friends in Christ*, 37.

response, however, was that my paper was too focused on us-versus-them. That helped me to focus on the importance of mutuality and the need for the newcomers to move from guest to host. The language of gifting was already a helpful start. The next piece of the puzzle came with the importance of the sacraments in the WCRC story, both in terms of the large number of baptisms in the last two years and the decision to hold the Lord's Supper weekly. This changed my focus to sacramental hospitality, especially the Eucharist. All these elements of hospitality are interrelated and reinforce one another. A further aspect of this movement from guest to host relates to the inclusion and the development of Farsi-speaking ordained leaders, which I will cover in the section on welcome and inclusion. Ordained leaders help a group in the congregation move solidly from guest to host and distributes the power in the church more evenly.

Kim Sun observes the importance of the exchange of gifts in mutuality and joy in his Mennonite perspective on hospitality. Though the practice of hospitality is important, if not done properly, it can create a "dichotomy between givers and receivers," and where hospitality can become a "paternalistic act where it heightens the position of the host, the giver, and characterize the guest as a passive receiver, where one's freedom and agency are denied."[128] A Farsi speaker shared in the intercultural group at WCRC that she did not want to be a guest forever. She wanted to contribute. Pohl warns, "There is a kind of hospitality that keeps people needy strangers while fostering an illusion of relationship and connection. It both disempowers and domesticates guests while it reinforces the host's power, control, and sense of generosity. It is profoundly destructive to the people it welcomes."[129] For Pohl, an important transformation occurs when the guest is empowered to become a host, and "their contributions can be recognized and when they are not first defined by their need."[130] Pohl notes that, for the host, this means a conscious decision to embrace marginality in order to make room for the guest.[131] This has been one way that the five English-speaking

---

128. Kim Sun, "Mennonite Perspective," 304.
129. Pohl, *Making Room*, 120.
130. Pohl, *Making Room*, 121.
131. Pohl, *Making Room*, 123.

Theological Reflection

leaders have welcomed their Farsi-speaking newcomers. However, for some in the congregation, it has been challenging to embrace such marginality, and it has led them to anxiety. We will cover this as one of the challenges to welcome. Developing friendship is another way for the host to embrace marginality and empower the guest.[132] This will continue to be a challenge for WCRC and so we turn to challenges to welcome.

CHALLENGES TO WELCOME

Challenges to welcome was the third most prevalent reference, after the English-speaking and Farsi-speaking church leaders. Its significance indicates that productive theological reflection can equip church leaders to address these challenges in both biblical and theological ways. This is particularly where the pastoral cycle of action and reflection and resulting action can help the congregation both be more aware of these challenges and make plans for overcoming these challenges with God's help. The challenges of language, culture, and Islamic influence are closely related, and so I will reflect theologically on these three challenges together. The last two challenges of busyness, anxiety, and resistance are different challenges. So, I will deal with them separately.

Language, Culture, and Islamic Influence

Language is key to any faith expression, and finding the right balance of Farsi language use and translation in Sunday services is a challenge. The use of English translation became an issue on Thursday evenings because of my presence in the Farsi Fellowship and my need for translation. Finding the right balance is key, but the use of a person's heart language in discipleship is foundational. Volf notes in *Exclusion and Embrace* that "before Babel the whole of humanity spoke *one* language; in Jerusalem the new community speaks *many* languages."[133] He says, when the Spirit comes, "each hears his or her own language spoken."[134] Volf then makes the important point that Pentecost does not revert the

---

132. Pohl, *Making Room*, 124.
133. Volf, *Exclusion and Embrace*, 228.
134. Volf, *Exclusion and Embrace*, 228.

church to the unity of cultural uniformity, but the unity is achieved "by advancing the harmony of cultural diversity."[135] When the members of WCRC do the hard work of patiently waiting through a long translation from Farsi to English, or a long stretch of English only, they are doing the hard work of honouring the work of the Spirit at Pentecost and allowing the Spirit to continue to work in the church at present. Volf points out that this harmony of cultural diversity, prophesized by Joel, is evident in the speech of daughters and slaves. The work of the Spirit in honouring diversity is followed by the believers sharing their possessions, and modelling distributive justice.[136] The justice of Pentecost "is indistinguishable from embrace: all have their needs met, and the deep desire of people to be themselves, to act in their own right, and yet to be understood are affirmed, are satisfied."[137] Unity and mutual care result from the Spirit's work in helping the Christian community appreciate cultural diversity. When WCRC does this hard work of linguistic and intercultural learning, they are fulfilling the prophesy of the prophet Joel and living out the meaning of Pentecost in our present day.

I will include the one mention of a negative experience of unwelcome here. As mentioned in the data findings, in one case, a Farsi speaker was nominated and put his name in for elder but was considered not sufficiently competent in speaking English to be able to be elected. This caused some humiliation for the individual and sadness on his part. This situation was exacerbated by a shame-based culture. This also occurred due to a misunderstanding and amid some tensions around ordaining Farsi-speaking elders. In this case, cultural sensitivity was needed on the part of the council and a humble spirit of learning and forgiveness on the part of the Farsi-speaking Iranians. Of course, this is not easy. As Pohl observes, "A life of hospitality is much less about dramatic gestures than it is about steady work— faithful labor that is undergirded by prayer and sustained by grace."[138] In a context like WCRC, with its significant cultural complexity, mistakes are bound to occur. While it is important to minimize mistakes through increased cultural sensitivity,

135. Volf, *Exclusion and Embrace*, 228.
136. Volf, *Exclusion and Embrace*, 229.
137. Volf, *Exclusion and Embrace*, 229.
138. Pohl, *Making Room*, 183.

Theological Reflection

there is also a need for grace and forgiveness. Thankfully, this is very evident. There is also a need for cultural awareness and humility. Pohl lists humility and a grateful spirit as important traits for the host.[139] Volf adds the need for wisdom in citing the conflict that occurred in Acts between the Hellenists and the Hebrews. In that case, the forces of conflict that sought to undo Pentecost were instead redirected by a desire to embrace—a desire shaped by the memory of Pentecost and their own identity.[140]

Cultural differences continue to pose a challenge for the unity of the church and for discipleship of the Farsi-speaking community. The cultural traits of *ta'arof*, patron–client relationships, shame and honour, and competition/jealousy make church discipleship a challenge. The Dutch Canadian culture is part of the WCRC culture and needs to be addressed as well if cultural differences are to be bridged.

Shame and honour paradigms are a challenging cultural dynamic for the church because the West has prioritized guilt and righteousness paradigms. Oksnevad observes the prevalence of shame and honour paradigms in Iranian communities. He writes that every culture has a mix of guilt/righteousness, honour/shame, and fear/power paradigms, but some cultures emphasize one or two.[141] Shame is an "internal pressure to behave in an honorable manner, the psychological drive to escape or prevent negative judgement by others."[142] Chronic shame can lead to avoidance or attacking others, conflict and hypersensitivity to perceived offences.[143] Evidently, such behaviours can cause troubles and challenge unity in any church fellowship. Mischke sees the impact of the gospel on people in a shame-and-honour paradigm because Christ's humiliation and exaltation are a shame–honour reversal. This motif within the grand narrative of Scripture brings hope to all who suffer from shame.[144] Believers in Jesus are saturated with the king's

---

139. Pohl, *Making Room*, 172.
140. Volf, *Exclusion and Embrace*, 230.
141. Oksnevad, *Burden of Baggage*, 44.
142. Oksnevad, *Burden of Baggage*, 45.
143. Oksnevad, *Burden of Baggage*, 46–47.
144. Mischke, *Global Gospel*, 274.

honour and the "believers have no honor deficit."[145] This is good news for all believers who are trapped in chronic shame.

Mischke also relates the gospel to patronage in cultures where this is significant, including patron–client relationships. This is clear in passages such as John 3:16, describing God's patronage and benefaction as a gift and grace of God to the believer.[146] Therefore, while Farsi-speaking Iranians may look to the leadership of WCRC council as patrons and benefactors, all believers can look to God as the ultimate patron and benefactor, one who is always faithful and caring for his people. This is an opportunity not only to focus on the Iranian community but also to celebrate—as a community—God's gracious patronage of his children and his healing of shame and restoring of honour. This kind of theological perspective increases unity and mutuality.

Related to shame and honour is the Iranian experience of trauma. Although this did not come up often in interviews because I carefully avoided re-traumatizing the informants, Parmida did make one reference to this issue, saying, "Their souls are injured in many ways. They have experienced trauma in many ways." Trauma and its effects on the Farsi-speaking community are important for the leadership of WCRC to recognize and understand. Trauma and shame-and-honour issues are related because shame may lead to a hesitancy to name trauma and seek treatment. Oksnevad observed trauma in his study among Iranians who were "spiritually, emotionally and sometimes physically wounded."[147] Menakem writes about how trauma can be carried in the body and how it can come out later through traumatic retention.[148] Bringing healing to traumatized individuals through Jesus' example of healing and compassion will need to be an ongoing component of discipleship at WCRC. Jesus' death on the cross allows for forgiveness and healing by conquering evil. In that sense, the Trauma Healing Institute of the American Bible Society (traumahealinginstitute.org) is a good resource.

---

145. Mischke, *Global Gospel*, 324.
146. Mischke, *Global Gospel*, 252.
147. Oksnevad, *Burden of Baggage*, 155.
148. Menakem, *My Grandmother's Hands*, 54–55.

Theological Reflection

Many of the Farsi converts who attend WCRC do not have close ties to Islam. Some described it as part of their cultural background. Informants did note that cultural influences are significant and can be a challenge in discipling new believers. Diba described that the process was like learning a guitar but with the wrong method. The method had to be unlearned, and a new method should be used to replace the old if one wanted to play it well. Von Kaehne also noted in their Iranian community that ties to Islam were weak but that there were "patterns of thought such as works versus grace and leadership models" that needed attention in the process of Christian discipleship.[149] That points to the challenges of discipling Persian believers who still are influenced by Islamic culture and thoughts. Little recommends welcoming individuals from an Islamic background "into vital Spirit-filled groups of believers which are experiencing the realities of the new covenant together."[150] Nikoo mentioned that many of the new believers were tired of the restrictions imposed on them in Iran by religious authorities. Oksnevad believes that the renewing of the mind (Rom 12:1–2) and putting on a new self in Christ (Eph 4:22–24) are important for the transition from Islam to Christianity.[151] One of the goals of the Farsi Fellowship is to provide opportunities to volunteer and gain real life experience serving as a disciple. Little notes the importance of reducing family pressure on converts to revert to Islam and of supporting the new believer through the church family.[152] This seemed to be less of a problem in the Farsi-speaking community at WCRC because many had left family and Islamic ties behind in Iran. One place where I observed this pressure was when they were in the need of safety and security, especially online. The Farsi-speaking Iranians had a high need for safety and security. The church as a family becomes more important when you have lost your family due to immigration or rejection. The church as a family can function as an important protector and supporter.

Another Islamic cultural influence on the Farsi Fellowship I noticed during my participant observation was a tendency among the

---

149. von Kaehne, "Iranian Diaspora Ministry," 445.
150. Little, *Effective Discipling*, 72.
151. Oksnevad, *Burden of Baggage*, 93.
152. Little, *Effective Discipling*, 179.

believers to pursue allegorical explanations for Genesis. As a leader, Adel continually brought the group back to a more literal-historical method of exegesis. This caused some tension in the group during my observation period. This is an example of Islamic influences impacting the teaching and discipleship of new believers. Little, in studying methods of discipleship with new believers from an Islamic background, writes that adopting a new identity as a Christian and rejecting their old identity as a Muslim is important.[153] In this transition, Little notes that "the spiritual change that has taken place in the BMB (Believer from a Muslim Background) needs the strong support of a loving and caring Christian family to nurture and sustain their new identity."[154] Both the Farsi Fellowship and WCRC have provided this strong, loving, and supportive community. The developing identity as the family of God in WCRC is helpful for the long-term transition from Islam to Christianity.

One other cultural phenomenon mentioned by Parmida was the prevalence of competition and jealousy in the Farsi Fellowship. Nikoo also mentioned competition and jealousy, referring to it as "competition stuff." Oksnevad observes this cultural challenge in Iranian fellowships. Oksnevad concludes that many Iranian believers suffer from PTSD, "having been spiritually, emotionally and sometimes physically wounded."[155] This trauma has also led to much suspicion, fear, and a survival mentality among believers, which then cause "survival of the fittest" behaviour. This could explain the competition and jealousy among Farsi-speaking members. Oksnevad found in interviews that the informants were suspicious, looking for ulterior motives. This again points to the importance of the Iranian members' trauma in the WCRC context. Could embodied hospitality in this context involve making space for trauma healing and emotional and spiritual health? The gospel is good news for the broken hearted, and Jesus says in Matt 5:4, "Blessed are those who mourn for they will be comforted" (NIV). Rebekah Eklund points out that this Beatitude allows for broad interpretive range, drawing on Israel's exile, which evokes "a wide variety

---

153. Little, *Effective Discipling*, 189.
154. Little, *Effective Discipling*, 196.
155. Oksnevad, *Burden of Baggage*, 155.

of griefs (the potential loss of the covenant with God, foreign dominations, starvation, loss of land and home, death)."[156] Such a long list of griefs would be a helpful reminder to the Iranian members that God cares for them and that mourning is part of the healing process.

There is a rich biblical witness of God caring for the refugee and the alien and bringing healing and restoration to those who mourn. Langmead observes, "Jesus constantly broke boundaries and reversed the social order in affirming the human dignity and blessedness of those on the margins of this society—the women, children, ritually impure, poor, sick, cultural outsiders, and moral failures."[157] Jesus' message is relevant to refugees on the margins because it is "good news for those who are persecuted as justice seekers" (Matt 5:10) and for those who are poor, who weep now and are hungry (Luke 6:21).[158] Jesus centred himself in a rich Hebrew tradition of God's mercy and justice. God is a "refuge for the oppressed, a place of safety in times of trouble" (Ps 9:9).[159] Oksnevad provides a solution to the problem of competition and jealousy through a God-directed service model, which requires a major shift in worldview. Creating healthy boundaries, developing transparency, and an ability to be vulnerable are also important.[160]

Busyness, Anxiety, and Resistance

Pohl notes that, in today's busy world, people have limited time to practice hospitality. Yet this stands in tension with a world in which many people are on the move and churches are called to offer a compassionate response.[161] In the case of WCRC, the older English-speaking members have capacity and time for hospitality, but their guests, the Farsi-speaking Iranians, are very busy. This was mentioned several times. Becoming established in a new country takes a lot of time and energy. Diba shared that he was working on construction twelve hours a day. This made it hard to be a part of church activities despite his desire to be

156. Eklund, *Beatitudes*, 104.
157. Langmead, "Refugees as Guests and Hosts," 34.
158. Langmead, "Refugees as Guests and Hosts," 35.
159. Langmead, "Refugees as Guests and Hosts," 35.
160. Oksnevad, *Burden of Baggage*, 156.
161. Pohl, *Making Room*, 151.

involved. The reality for newcomers to Canada is that the challenges are numerous—from learning English, to obtaining a driver's license, to securing credentials for a professional career, or to going back to school for further education. One Farsi speaker served as a deacon for a year but then needed to resign to pursue professional credentials. Many of the Farsi-speaking Iranians continued to participate in the Farsi Fellowship because it was on Zoom. Having a mix of in-person and Zoom meetings could help with the challenges of balancing so many competing activities with the need for discipleship. Farsi-speaking Iranians who wanted to attend church could find rides to the church through Adel and Parmida.

Pohl wisely observes, "When strangers are welcomed in, especially if they come in significant numbers, or if they are quite different from the welcoming community, there will be strains on identity."[162] This has been the case at WCRC, where a congregation of seventy to eighty members has welcomed a Farsi-speaking community of one-hundred-and-fifty people. It is also true that Iranian culture is significantly different from both Canadian culture and the Dutch Canadian sub-culture. It is not surprising that there were some references to anxiety and resistance among the English-speaking older members. They have absorbed a lot of change in the midst of a destabilizing global pandemic. For this reason, the response needs to be pastoral. Pohl notes that when "strangers stay long term or desire to join the community, then a fairly complex set of questions about beliefs and behaviors emerge."[163]

Pullenayegem's observations on congregational anxiety in the face of change could be helpful to WCRC at this point. The first kind of anxiety is survival anxiety and the second is learning anxiety.[164] Survival anxiety comes with remaining the same while learning anxiety is associated with change.[165] The congregation was undergoing survival anxiety in the midst of congregational decline when the first Farsi-speaking Iranians arrived. They are now experiencing learning anxiety as they cope with change. As was mentioned by one informant, this

162. Pohl, *Making Room*, 141.
163. Pohl, *Making Room*, 141.
164. Pullenayegem, "Surviving or Thriving?" 182.
165. Pullenayegem, "Surviving or Thriving?" 182.

may increase as the congregation returns from Zoom services and better appreciates how the congregation has changed. Pullenayegem recommends reducing the learning anxiety by helping people focus on the new environment, inviting them to experience and experiment with the new reality so that they realize that change is not so bad after all.[166] He helpfully notes, "Disruption is God's way of transforming the church."[167] This can be helpful because disruption can "precipitate creative re-imaging and innovative practices."[168]

Two helpful examples are Rønsdal's idea of the "call to mend creation" and the notion of cultural humility in Captari, Shannonhouse, J. N. Hook, Aten, E. Davis, D. Davis, Van Tongeren, and J. R. Hook. Rønsdal notes that in the face of resistance to accepting and welcoming refugees, the concept of "calling" is a helpful idea to motivate believers to action. God *calls* his people to welcome the refugee, and this is part of the role of the believer "to assist God in the mending of creation."[169] Captari and her co-authors observed that those who were most able to receive Syrian refugees had cultivated cultural humility.[170] Such cultural humility was evident in the leaders who exhibited welcome as a *habitus*.

Finally, Volf's reflections on Pentecost are applicable to this situation. In Pentecost, Babel is undone, not through cultural and linguistic uniformity but through diversity.[171] The multicultural dimension of the church is God's vision for the church today. The call to the church today is to embrace this vision despite the challenges and the discomfort that come through disorientation and reorientation. The good news is that this is the work of the Holy Spirit, and the Spirit is present in the church today and in WCRC. The Spirit is leading this change and will help those who are struggling with this change to adapt, if they stay in step with the Spirit.

---

166. Pullenayegem, "Surviving or Thriving?" 182.
167. Pullenayegem, "Surviving or Thriving?" 183.
168. Pullenayegem, "Surviving or Thriving?" 183.
169. Rønsdal, "We Were Invited to Friendships," 30.
170. Captari et al., "Prejudicial and Welcoming Attitudes," 135.
171. Volf, *Exclusion and Embrace*, 128.

FROM WELCOME TO INCLUSION

Van Opstal notes three key moves in forming a diverse fellowship. First is hospitality where the key phrase is "We welcome you." The next is solidarity whose key phrase is "We stand with you." The third move is mutuality where the key phrase is "We need you." Three ways that the church has sought to move from hospitality to mutuality is through servant leadership, volunteer opportunities, and electing Farsi-speaking Iranians to ordained leadership.

Adel and Parmida have intentionally adopted a servant-leadership model for the Farsi Fellowship in contrast to many Farsi ministries that tend to stress the authority of the leader. In this servant-leader approach, they were being countercultural to normal Iranian practices. Oksnevad found in his research of Iranian fellowships that "pastoral leadership often reflects high control and authoritarian rule, replicating a familial system in Iran."[172] Adel and Parmida were convinced they were following a better biblical model. Jesus stresses that his followers must be servants who put the other first. In Mark 9:35, Jesus says to the twelve disciples, "Whoever wants to be first must be last of all and servant of all" (NRSV). Oksnevad notes that many Iranian pastors are bi-vocational and do not have time to attend to all the responsibilities of ministry.[173] Adel and Parmida are also bi-vocational but have been able to give sufficient pastoral attention to the Farsi Fellowship. Being one unified church has helped them in having other English-speaking leaders supporting them in their ministry and encouraging them on a regular basis.

Adel and Parmida adopted another strategy for welcome and inclusion—it was to look for volunteer opportunities so that the Farsi-speaking Iranians could use their gifts in the service of the church as quickly as possible. The Farsi-speaking Iranians all appreciated the opportunity to use their gifts in the congregation and felt useful in being allowed to become involved in different church activities. Such inclusion encouraged them as newcomers in a country where they face many barriers and their experience may not always include being

---

172. Oksnevad, *Burden of Baggage*, 110.
173. Oksnevad, *Burden of Baggage*, 110.

appreciated. In the church, they could feel needed and that they belonged. Paul speaks of the importance of spiritual gifts in 1 Cor 12:1. WCRC is being revitalized because the Farsi-speaking members are being encouraged to use their gifts in the church.

In the case of ordained leadership for the Farsi-speaking Iranians, the church council pushed to have Farsi-speaking Iranians as elders and deacons as soon as possible. This created some tension because Adel and Parmida felt that the Farsi-speaking Iranians had not developed sufficient spiritual maturity to take on formal leadership roles. A further complication was that the Farsi-speaking Iranians needed a certain level of competence in English to function well on the council. Despite these tensions, it is clear that the church has benefited from having ordained elders and deacons who can speak Farsi on each pastoral district of the church. Ordaining leaders allows the Farsi-speaking leaders to respond to pastoral situations in culturally sensitive ways. This has brought more mutuality to church leadership. One of the challenges within the Farsi community was the cultural trait of competition and jealousy that made it hard for anyone to rise in the community to these positions. Another challenge was the cultural deference shown to older members of the community, which, however, was often not extended to an ordained leader perceived as being young. Despite the challenges, the council is supporting Volf's views on inclusion and embrace. Volf believes that "God's reception of hostile humanity into divine communion is a model for how human beings should relate to the other."[174] For Volf, the cross is all about God breaking the power of human enmity without violence in order to welcome human beings into divine communion.[175] Such embrace also demonstrates God's Trinitarian welcome, especially seen in Jesus' open arms on the cross that welcomes all.[176] This is something that churches can and should embrace. WCRC is overcoming natural enmity between people of different ethnicity and culture by embracing ordained leadership of the Farsi-speaking Iranians. Paul counsels Timothy to "let no one despise

---

174. Volf, *Exclusion and Embrace*, 100.
175. Volf, *Exclusion and Embrace*, 126.
176. Volf, *Exclusion and Embrace*, 128.

your youth" (1 Tim 4:12), and this is helpful advice for those Farsi-speaking elders and deacons who feel inadequate in this new role.

EFFECTS OF SOCIAL CONTACT AND IDENTITY

Social contact and identity theory presupposes that groups that have increased contact with each other will grow together and overcome prejudice and misconceptions. Groups that go through the process of contact can also grow together positively when they adopt a superordinate identity. The foundational theological principle is that all human beings are made in the image of God. Genesis 1:27 says, "So, God created humankind in his image, in the image of God he created them; male and female he created them" (NRSV). People already have something in common before they meet in social contact in the church. Followers of Jesus have a further bond in that they are *adopted children* of God by the Spirit of adoption and are part of God's family (Rom 8:15). In coming together as God's family in the church, Paul says in Gal 3:28 that there is "no longer Jew or Greek; there is no longer slave or free, there is no longer male or female; for all of you are one in Christ Jesus" (NRSV). Added to the social effects of contact is the work of the Holy Spirit that brings unity even among people who are significantly different. This same Spirit also gives us a common identity as followers of Jesus. When I asked some of the Farsi-speaking informants about their primary identities, they identified themselves, most of all, as followers of Jesus. They were also committed to being members of WCRC, which, too, gave them a shared, superordinate identity that strengthened the bonds of the church, making them stronger than the bonds of nation.

One of the strengths of WCRC in identity formation is the many baptisms that have established the identity of the believer as a child of God. The weekly practice of holding the Lord's Supper, too, reinforces that identification with Christ. The sacraments play a key role in the formation and maintenance of a superordinate identity that is so important. Ammerman calls rituals such as baptism and the Lord's Supper "rites of intensification." These are rites that "intensify the group's commitments to its shared beliefs and meanings."[177] One of the

---

177. Ammerman, "Cultural and Identity," 86.

Theological Reflection

challenges that WCRC faced was that the COVID-19 pandemic had meant that there were far fewer opportunities to gather around food for fellowship and social contact. Social contact theory would encourage regular social gatherings between different cultural groups, which had been a common phenomenon before the pandemic (e.g., the *Nowruz* celebration). Despite the limitations of the pandemic, friendships have formed. Such friendships reduce anxiety and prejudice as others in the community observe such cross-cultural friendships. COVID-19 isolation presented challenges to the public nature of friendship and may have blunted the full effect of this social theory. However, the existence of such friendships is a hopeful sign. The benefits of such intergroup friendships are noted by Ortiz and Harwood and are an important part of growing mutuality at WCRC.[178] Vezzali and Stathi also write about the benefits of intergroup friendship.[179] Captari, Shannonhouse, J. N. Hook, Aten, E. Davis, D. Davis, Van Tongeren, and J. R. Hook, in referring to engagement with refugees, note that "genuine closeness and meaningful relationships across group boundaries" are helpful for encouraging engagement. Such engagement also encourages more mutuality in the relationship.[180] In terms of refugee engagement, WCRC has created genuine closeness and meaningful relationships across group boundaries, which point to the culture of hospitality and the work of the Spirit in preparing the congregation for welcoming the stranger.

One other challenge in the formation of group identity is that, when two groups meet, there is a need to differentiate themselves, presenting themselves to the other and explaining "the kinds of person they are."[181] This is because individuals and groups need to balance "standing outside of" and "belonging to" the group. This is the tension between inclusiveness and distinctiveness.[182] In this case, each group needs to have an opportunity to be heard and to share about their culture, their history, and their values. For example, Farsi-speaking Iranians often mention how important poetry is in their culture. This *need*

---

178. Oritz and Harwood, "Social Cognitive Theory," 628.
179. Vezzali and Stathi, "Extended Intergroup Contact Hypothesis," 116.
180. Captari et al., "Prejudicial and Welcoming Attitudes," 135.
181. Moghaddam, *Multiculturalism and Intergroup Relations*, 91.
182. Moghaddam, *Multiculturalism and Intergroup Relations*, 101.

to be heard applies to both the newer Farsi-speaking Iranians and the older English speakers. It is important that each group listens actively to the other, and that opportunities exist for this kind of sharing. One of the dangers is that one group assumes something about the other—for example, the English-speaking group may assume that the immigration experience of the Farsi-speaking Iranians is like that of the Dutch members. While there may be some superficial similarities, on a deeper level, they are quite different experiences. Baptisms present an opportunity for stories of the believers to be circulated and shared among the church members. It also functions as a rite of intensification to reorient social identity towards a new superordinate identity—members of the church of Christ. Such a community now supersedes all other communities, cultures, and gods, according to Volf.[183] It also happens in the post-sermon discussion time when both English- and Farsi-speaking Iranians can ask questions and discuss ideas together. Opportunities to share happen informally around table fellowship and in homes, which was something that WCRC had been practicing before the pandemic.

Tajfel notes that an individual's image or concept of him- or herself is complex. The main point is that some of an individual's self-images derive from the social group, especially if there is high salience.[184] While it is hard to evaluate self-image, social behaviour can be observed.[185] As WCRC contributes to the positive aspects of both the English-speaking and the Farsi-speaking Iranian persons' identity, it will encourage cohesion. Such cohesion will be evident through combined social activities involving in-groups and out-groups. Tajfel observed that individuals can remain if they are able to reinterpret the salience of the group or work towards change (increasing status, for example).[186] At any time, there will be individuals in different stages of identity change and formation. The key application for WCRC is that all are transformed in their relationships with Christ into a new identity. As this important spiritual truth is emphasized in the community through rites of intensification, it will help with group cohesion.

183. Volf, *Exclusion and Embrace*, 40.
184. Tajfel, *Human Groups and Social Categories*, 255.
185. Tajfel, *Human Groups and Social Categories*, 255.
186. Tajfel, *Human Groups and Social Categories*, 256.

Theological Reflection

Allport felt that religion was a paradox when it came to prejudice. Religion can both increase prejudice and reduce it. In *The Nature of Prejudice*, he describes two kinds of religiosity reflected in an unpublished experiment. For individuals who are devout and personally invested in their religion, prejudice was reduced. For those for whom religion was more institutional—about political stances or the social activities of the religion—prejudice increased.[187] The potential application for WCRC is that faith formation will also benefit social relationships that can be further enhanced through social contact.

GOD AT WORK

A belief in God's sovereign work was apparent in many of the informants' answers. It became clear that Pastor Aaron believed he was moved by the Spirit to begin talking about his Emmaus Road vision to prepare the congregation to welcome the stranger and to be open to what God might do in the context of a declining congregation. Not long after, Adel and Parmida felt led to come to WCRC and felt immediately at peace. They brought with them a whole network of Farsi-speaking Iranians from their Persian ministry with global connections. The stories of both the English speakers and the Farsi-speaking Iranians pointed to God who was at work in bringing them to WCRC and helping them to feel at home there.

Branson and Roxburgh believe that we should be attentive to what God is doing in the world and that "God engages a world that has been turned upside down and we need our own lenses to be flipped, or we miss what God is doing and thereby we lose opportunities to participate in turning it right-side up."[188]

One story that emerged out of my contact with the Farsi Fellowship was an individual who had visited WCRC and felt the peace and love of God immediately. He became a Christian and returned to Iran where he led his wife to become a Christian, and then they decided to immigrate to Canada and become members of WCRC. Stories like that are part of the renewal that is happening at WCRC, and they point to God at work. Among the Farsi-speaking Iranians, there is a strong

---

187. Allport, *Nature of Prejudice*, 421.
188. Branson and Roxburgh, *Leadership*, 32.

belief in miracles, and as a community, they witness to God's power in the present. Though they face many challenges in leaving behind a country and culture that which they love, they also have hope for what God can do for them to ensure their future in Canada. Their presence at WCRC is a part of that hope.

Heather shared in an interview that WCRC was becoming more aware of the Spirit's work in their congregation. She observed that one of the benefits of the Farsi speaker's presence was awakening to the movement of the Spirit. She said, "I think the other benefit of this is to actually wake up and say, 'Are we partnering with what the Spirit is doing? Or are we just perpetuating what we want to do?'" WCRC is experiencing renewal through the presence of God in the stranger.

SUMMARY

There is much to theologically reflect on in this story of hospitality at WCRC. That is because the foundation of hospitality is in God's Trinitarian nature and in Christ's death and resurrection. Christ's open arms beckon all to come, and this has been embodied in the WCRC context. This embodied hospitality is evident not only in the special role of the seven church leaders but also in the acceptance of this welcome and the mutual give-and-take of hospitality between host and guest that has developed at WCRC. This growing mutuality is a direct result of the decision to be one unified church. One unified church has led to the rich gifts of God's people benefiting all in a diverse congregation. Those Holy Spirit-inspired gifts of diversity are evident in the gifts of the Farsi-speaking Iranians and English speakers at WCRC. The sacraments of baptism and the Lord's Supper have played a strong role in the experience of welcome. What has solidified the welcome of newcomers at WCRC has been intentional and unintentional (*habitus*) practices of inclusion such as ordaining Farsi-speaking elders and deacons. There have been challenges to welcome and inclusion, and those challenges continue. But identification of these challenges and theological reflection is helpful in finding solutions. Social contact theory and social identity theory point to the benefits of increased contact and a unified identity and that are born out in the congregation. God is clearly at work. Despite the limitations of a case study such as this, there are clearly principles of welcome that can be shared with other congregational contexts. The potential of this research project, limitations of this study, and possible further study will be discussed in the final chapter.

Chapter 6

Concluding Thoughts

WE HAVE MOVED FROM experience and exploration to reflection, and now we turn to action. How does what we have learned apply to the continuing culture and practice of welcome at WCRC and other Christian Reformed churches that are encountering the other in a changing world where many are on journeys of global migration? What are the implications for the church in Canada today, and how can these findings be helpful on a larger scale? I now return to the original research problem and thesis statement and discuss emergent understanding for the missional church, the multicultural church, and the church that seeks to provide hospitality to the stranger.

The main research problem that this book has examined is the welcome and inclusion of a group of strangers from a very different culture and background into a Christian Reformed congregation. The thesis is that there are visible and discernable practices and rituals of embodied hospitality and inclusion that can be both observed and reflected upon. These practices and rituals, forming together a culture of welcome and *habitus*, can be helpful for further refinement of practice in the context of WCRC (action stage) as well as Christian Reformed churches and churches of other denominations in Canada who exist in diverse contexts.

Such application comes with the caution that this is a case study of a Canadian congregation. In this way, the findings reflect a very specific constellation of events that God has engineered at WCRC so that

Concluding Thoughts

the Farsi-speaking Iranians could find a warm welcome and a home at a Christian Reformed church made up of older immigrants from the Netherlands. This is a unique situation and a work of the Spirit. But we can also speak of postures and practices that could be applied to other church settings. The posture of cultural humility and seeing the other as a gift (referring to both guest and host) are evident at WCRC and could be applied to other churches. Practices such as forming one unified body of Christ, weekly celebration of the Lord's Supper, servant leadership, and ordination of different ethnic and linguistic groups into offices of the church can be applied to different contexts as well. Let us review the key findings.

KEY FINDINGS

One of the key findings of this study is that a few leaders were able to welcome a large group of strangers from a Persian cultural background in a few short years. This was possible because of the intentional and unintentional efforts in the form of *habitus*. This included both English- and Farsi-speaking leaders who extended hospitality to newcomers. The decision to be one church and not form separate congregations was also significant. It is helpful that the Farsi-speaking Iranians hold a separate meeting that is only in Farsi (unless English speakers are present as guests) for community and discipleship. Parmida is a gifted translator—together with Adel—and has many connections in the global Persian community. It would not be easy to replicate the experience of hospitality and welcome observed at WCRC without them. God has clearly been at work in bringing this configuration of individuals together.

Some practices stand out; however, that may prove useful to other church leaders. The decision to move to weekly Lord's Supper provided a moving ritual of welcome that transcended language for the Farsi-speaking Iranians, especially newcomers. As one informant expressed it, it is God who welcomes us to his table, and this is something that is both seen and felt in the sacrament, which is a good example of Eucharistic hospitality. Another practice related to the sacraments was the decision to baptize all who requested baptism without questioning motives. This is complicated in the case of Iranian newcomers because a letter from the church and certificate of baptism may be helpful for the successful outcome of a refugee claimant's hearing. It was felt that questioning motives was not biblical, nor did it follow Reformed tradition. They decided it was better to leave this question between the baptismal candidate and God. The sacraments were an important avenue of welcome at WCRC with over one hundred and twenty baptisms in the last three years and weekly Lord's Supper.

It became clear that Farsi-speaking Iranians were looking for specific things in a church—for example, safety and security, refugee hearing support, family, and an opportunity to learn Canadian culture and become more competent in the English language. WCRC was able to provide this as a gift to the Farsi-speaking community. This would have been much harder to do if they had formed their own congregation. WCRC benefited from the Farsi-speaking Iranians. They were a gift to the church in a period of decline as the congregation aged and many young people left due to the high cost of living in the North York area of Toronto. The Farsi-speaking Iranians provided church renewal through their youth, inspiration, baptism and testimony, and their vibrant faith and warm culture. There was an exchange of gifts that continued as they experienced hospitality, solidarity, and mutuality with each other. They would not have been able to exchange these gifts to this extent if they had remained separate congregations.

WCRC was intentional about moving from welcome to inclusion. They did this through a servant-leadership model which significantly differed from common Iranian models of leadership. Adel and Parmida quickly identified people's gifts and found opportunities for volunteer involvement in the church. They also provided opportunities for social events, picnics, backgammon tournaments, and *Nowruz* celebrations. In this way, they were able to provide a family-like social support system for people who had left family behind in Iran. They also worked together to ordain Farsi-speaking elders and deacons to church office. This process was not without its own challenges but English- and Farsi-speaking leaders worked together to make this happen by God's grace.

Being one unified church did bring significant challenges. The ongoing challenge of language continues to need creative solutions. I felt impatient while waiting through a long translation and had trouble

Concluding Thoughts

at times sustaining focus during the participant observation phase. The members of WCRC have been committed to including Farsi in the Sunday service at key points such as the congregational prayer, some worship songs, and the Apostles' Creed. Outlines of the sermon are distributed to the Farsi-speaking members as a helpful tool, and the sermon is dubbed into Farsi after it is delivered and posted on Telegram. There is a continuing debate as to whether simultaneous translation could be a helpful solution, but at this point, the congregation is finding their way with a level of translation that they are comfortable with. There have been misunderstandings due to cultural differences, but overall, both sides seek to be culturally sensitive and are learning from each other.

The rate of change has been high for this congregation although it is helpful that the Farsi-speaking newcomers did not come all at once but rather slowly over the last three years. Still, this has caused some anxiety in the older English-speaking members of the congregation. Their church is changing quickly and taking on an Iranian flavour which was nonexistent a few years ago. Managing this anxiety will be key for continued growth and development. The busyness of the Iranian community has also been a challenge. All immigrants face challenges in coming to a new country, and the Dutch CRC members experienced such challenges when they had arrived in Canada after World War II. While the older Dutch CRC members can relate to the challenges of immigration, there are significant differences when compared to the Iranian population, many of whom are refugee claimants, fleeing a repressive government where in some cases they have suffered persecution, and who also come from a pervasive Islamic culture. It is important that cultural sensitivity and an openness to learning about the other continue to develop and even form a new *habitus*.

This present growth of the Farsi Fellowship did not develop out of a vacuum but rather resulted from a long-term culture of welcome at WCRC. It is important to note that much of the welcome arose from a *habitus* of welcome exhibited by present leaders of the church. The church continues to build on this strength through the Farsi-speaking Iranians who have a strong culture of hospitality. Cultural differences will continue to present a challenge to the unity of the congregation.

Iranian culture involves such cultural traits as *ta'arof*, honour-shame dynamics, patron–client relationships, and latent Islamic influences. It is helpful that Adel and Parmida are experienced ministry leaders. The next challenge will be how to support and encourage their ministry within the WCRC congregation while also building more ties with the Farsi-speaking community through forming and discipling new leaders. Dutch Canadian culture involves a straight-forward form of communication that is very different from *ta'arof*. Bridging these cultural differences in the Spirit of Christ will continue to be important.

It is important to note that God has worked in very specific and unique ways to bring this situation together. Of course, God can do all things, but it is worth noting how special this situation is. WCRC leaders were obedient to God's call to welcome the stranger and God brought strangers to them from Iran. Many factors came together to make this an inspiring story. The Holy Spirit is at work at WCRC. He continues to work through his English speaking and Farsi speaking servants.

LIMITATIONS AND AREAS FOR FUTURE RESEARCH

This research project took place during the COVID-19 global pandemic. While I had hoped to do in-person interviews, the Omicron variant prevented that (late 2021 and early 2022). The advantage of doing Zoom interviews was that it was easy to get high-quality transcripts through the EnjoyHQ program. Thankfully, restrictions eased enough that I was able to follow my COVID-19 protocols and attend in-person Sunday services for four weeks. Farsi Fellowship meetings on Thursday continued to meet via Zoom, and I continued my once-per-month teaching sessions with the Farsi Fellowship. I documented references in interviews to pre-pandemic activities as well as limited activities during the pandemic. The elderly English-speaking population was more hesitant to return to in-person services even after the restrictions were lifted. Their hesitancy continued as there was talk of another COVID-19 wave in the fall of 2022.

Another limitation, specifically as an ethnographic project, was the length of the study period. I pursued this research during a three-month sabbatical from my role as a Diaspora Ministry Leader for

Concluding Thoughts

Resonate Global Mission. COVID-19 protocols and other delays meant that my MREB application was not approved until the middle of January 2022, so the actual length of this study ran from mid-January until the end of March, a period of two and a half months. I am thankful to the council of WCRC and the leaders of the Farsi Fellowship for their full support of this study.

Due to my decision to use James Spradley's ethnographic research method and time limitations, I chose eight informants (one more was added for a total of nine as a guarantee in case someone dropped out) and interviewed each informant three times. While qualitative research is more about saturation—something that I approached through multiple interviews—it would be beneficial to speak with even more members of the congregation about their experience. Most of my volunteers were current leaders or had been involved in leadership in the past. This may have been because I chose those who volunteered first as part of my MREB consent protocol and so gathered those who were most committed to hospitality and welcome in the church. This could give the study an overly positive perspective. This was the reason that I documented two experiences of "unwelcome."

With these limitations in mind, it would be beneficial to do a longer-term ethnographic study of a church like WCRC. It would also be interesting to do a study of another ethnic group that has become a part of an existing church in Canada and compare the experience and culture. It would also be helpful to do a comparative study with another Canadian congregation that has absorbed a notable number of Farsi-speaking Iranians. It seems that, as Canadian culture becomes more diverse, there will be more opportunities for congregational studies of this nature. The fast-growing Iranian church today should also provide more opportunities to study this particular ethnic group as it grows in Canada.

Another area for research would be to explore some of the themes in this book that have stood out and to gain a deeper understanding of them. One study could look at how many churches have accepted ethnic communities from different cultures into their fellowships as opposed to rental agreements and parallel congregational life. If congregations do exist side by side in the same building, do they come together for any events? A theme that became important was sacramental hospitality. One future study could look at elements of the Lord's Supper as hospitality to strangers from other ethnic and cultural communities. Baptism as initiation into the church is another rich area of research into sacramental hospitality. It would benefit this study to gain further insight into the challenges of immigration and to examine how the church supports refugees and immigrants throughout the immigration process. This could involve both ethnographic and phenomenological methodologies to understand the experience of refugee claimants to Canada and their relationship to the church. This would be a complex study because there are many pressures on new immigrants. It would be helpful to trace this journey further once Iranian believers are settled in Canada and to evaluate how the next generation is being included in the church. It would also be fruitful to know more about the lives of other ethnic communities and their experience in the church. The face of the church in Canada is changing and knowledge of how it is changing would be relevant.

My ability to reflect on the role of social contact in the coming together of two very different cultural groups and to reflect on the importance of the two groups forming one identity was limited. My research questions were mainly focused on the culture and experience of welcome, and so attitudes and prejudices were difficult to evaluate. It could be helpful to do further study around social contact and identity theories and congregational cohesion. Churches can benefit from knowing how to reduce prejudice and negative attitudes towards other groups. This could also help reduce anxiety and tensions in a congregation, absorbing many people from a different ethnic and cultural group. Interviewing the Farsi- and English-speaking informants was a very inspiring experience. I am thankful to have been able to listen to and share in stories of welcome and inclusion. There is a place for sharing these positive stories and inspiring other churches to embrace the stranger. Not only are these stories and the story of WCRC inspiring, but such stories also invite people to participate in what God is doing in the world today. I have heard anecdotal stories that such movements of people are happening in other denominations. I once attended a United Church of Canada service in Montreal and witnessed the baptism

Concluding Thoughts

of eighteen new Iranian Christians that Sunday. There was a spirit of renewal in that church as well, and evidence that God was at work. Such cross sharing of stories could be an encouragement to welcoming the stranger and could only help the mission of God today.

SUMMARY

This research project has sought to understand the culture of welcome, in terms of practices, rituals and embodied hospitality in the welcome of Farsi-speaking newcomers at WCRC. Specific practices were identified through interviews with informants. Some findings were surprising— such as the importance of a few welcoming leaders and the importance of sacramental hospitality. The importance of Eucharistic hospitality and the welcome embodied in weekly celebration of the Lord's Supper was an unexpected and helpful outcome of the study. Such hospitality also encourages mutuality as God welcomes us all to the table. Other findings— such as the challenge of language and cultural differences— were more of a concern. My hope is that WCRC will be encouraged by these findings while at the same time finding theological tools to help with the challenges identified.

The benefit of this research project has been in understanding this experience and the *habitus* of welcome, both to help this particular church continue to grow and develop as a multicultural community and to benefit other churches that find themselves in similar multicultural situations. As practices of welcome are encouraged or modified, further theological reflection can occur in this area of hospitality. While there are definite limitations of this study, significant insights were gained over the study period through a qualitative ethnographic methodology. There is potential for further research into hospitality towards Iranian newcomers and other populations who are migrating to Canada and becoming part of Canadian churches. This is a rich field of study, and I am thankful to have an opportunity to contribute to the knowledge and experience of embodied hospitality and welcome in this particular congregation of WCRC.

Appendix

Ethnographic Research Interview Questions

With ethnographic research and open-ended interview questions, it is recommended to prepare descriptive questions in advance. Then more advanced structural and contrast questions can be devised as the interview series proceeds. The following is an example of some of the descriptive, structural and contrast questions used in the interviews.

1. DESCRIPTIVE QUESTIONS

Descriptive questions are the first to be included in interviews to build semantic domains and begin to form taxonomies of cultural terms.

For English Speakers:

a. Can you describe a typical week in the life of Willowdale CRC?

b. In what ways have you contributed to the welcome of newcomers to Willowdale?

c. What have been some highlights for you of life in the Willowdale community?

d. Could you describe some welcoming events you have participated in?

APPENDIX

For Farsi-Speaking Iranians:

a. Can you describe an event at Willowdale where you felt welcome?

b. What have been some events that you have attended at Willowdale?

c. Can you describe any times you felt unwelcome?

d. Have there been people who helped you feel welcome into the congregation?

e. Can you describe parts of the worship service that make you feel welcome?

2. STRUCTURAL QUESTIONS

For English Speakers:

a. What are all the different kinds of activities at Willowdale that would welcome new people?

b. What are ways that you welcome people who speak Farsi or another language?

c. You mentioned Neighbour Link as a way to welcome people – is that from within your church or is it an outside organization? Do you partner with organizations from the community?

d. Is leadership on the council possible for Farsi-speaking Iranians?

For Farsi-Speaking Iranians:

a. Where have you found the most help in connecting to the church?

b. Is the Farsi Fellowship a separate congregation or part of Willowdale? How is it a part?

c. Have you had social and daily living needs met in the church? Spiritual needs? What takes priority?

Ethnographic Research Interview Questions

3. CONTRAST QUESTIONS

For English Speakers:

a. From this list of church activities (on cards) which are the most welcoming to Persian newcomers?

b. How is a Bible Study more welcoming than a worship service?

c. How are Farsi-speaking Iranians prepared for leadership and how does that differ from English speakers?

For Farsi-Speaking Iranians

a. From this list of church activities (on cards) which are the most welcoming to Persian newcomers?

b. How is a Bible study more welcoming than a worship service?

c. How are Farsi-speaking Iranians prepared for leadership and how does that differ from English speakers?

ADDITIONAL QUESTIONS
(ADDED AFTER THE FIRST SERIES OF INTERVIEWS):

1. Descriptive (for both English-speakers and Farsi-speaking Iranians):

    a. Could you describe your experience of welcome at Willowdale? How long ago was that? Were there any key people involved? Any important events?

    b. What are some of the benefits of welcoming the Iranian community into Willowdale CRC?

    c. What have been some of the challenges of welcoming the Iranian community into Willowdale?

2. Structural (for both English-speakers and Farsi-speaking Iranians):

    a. What are some characteristics of a welcoming person? Where do you see that at Willowdale? Has your perception of Legacy members/Iranians changed in any ways in the last year?

APPENDIX

    b How does welcome lead to inclusion?

    c. Where do you see Willowdale in 10 years? What is your vision for the future?

    d. How have the following affected (helped/hindered) the welcome of the other at Willowdale? Aging congregation/slow trickly growth/unified church/Farsi-English use.

    e. How have the newcomers led to revival at Willowdale?

    f. How have people adapted to so much change?

3. Contrast (for both English-speakers and Farsi-speaking Iranians):

    a. Do you notice any ways that welcome is different in the Farsi and English-speaking communities?

    b. Do you notice any difference in helping members socially or economically in the two communities?

    c. How much does shame play a role in helping the Farsi speaking community?

    d. Can you identify the most important element of welcome and why is it more important than the others we have talked about?

Bibliography

Abrams, Dominic, and Michael A. Hogg. "An Introduction to the Social Identity Approach." In *Social Identity Theory: Constructive and Critical Advances*, edited by Dominic Abrams and Michael A. Hogg, 1–9. New York: Springer, 1990.
Aldiabat, Khaldoun, et al. "The Lived Experience of Syrian Refugees in Canada: A Phenomenological Study." *The Qualitative Report* 26 (2021) 484–506.
Allport, Gordon W. *The Nature of Prejudice*. Garden City, NY: Doubleday, 1958.
Almedingen, E. M. *St. Francis of Assisi: A Great Life in Brief*. New York: A. A. Knopf, 1967.
Alvesson, Mats, and Kaj Sköldberg. *Reflexive Methodology: New Vistas for Qualitative Research*. London: Sage, 2018.
Ammerman, Nancy T. "Cultural and Identity in the Congregation." In *Studying Congregations: A New Handbook*, edited by Nancy T. Ammerman et al., 78–104. Nashville: Abingdon, 1998.
Ammerman, Nancy T., and Arthur E. Farnsley II. *Congregation and Community*. New Brunswick, NJ: Rutgers University Press, 1996.
Ballard, Paul, and John Pritchard. *Practical Theology in Action: Christian Thinking in the Service of Church and Society*. London: SPCK, 1996.
Baucum, Tory K. *Evangelical Hospitality: Catechetical Evangelism in the Early Church and its Recovery for Today*. Lanham, MD: Scarecrow, 2008.
Bavinck, Herman. *Reformed Dogmatics: Holy Spirit, Church, and New Creation*, edited by John Bolt. Translated by John Vriend. Grand Rapids: Baker Academic, 2008.
Beach, Lee. *The Church in Exile: Living in Hope after Christendom*. Downers Grove, IL: InterVarsity, 2015.
Beasley-Murray, G. R. *Baptism in the New Testament*. Grand Rapids: Eerdmans, 1962.

Bibliography

Berkhof, L. *Systematic Theology*. 1939. Reprint, Grand Rapids: Eerdmans, 1988.

Bethune, Pierre-Francois de. *Interreligious Hospitality: The Fulfillment of Dialogue*. Collegeville, PA: Liturgical Press, 2010.

Bibby, Reginald W. *Beyond the Gods and Back: Religion's Demise and Rise and Why It Matters*. Lethbridge, AB: Project Canada, 2011.

———. *Restless Gods: The Renaissance of Religion in Canada*. Toronto: Stoddart, 2002.

Bock, Darrell L. *Luke*. The New NIV Application Commentary. Grand Rapids: Zondervan, 1996.

Boersma, Hans, and Matthew Levering, eds. *The Oxford Handbook of Sacramental Theology*. Oxford: Oxford University Press, 2015.

Branson Mark L., and Juan F. Martinez. *Churches, Cultures and Leadership: A Practical Theology of Congregations and Ethnicities*. Downers Grove, IL: InterVarsity, 2011.

Branson Mark L., and Alan J. Roxburgh. *Leadership, God's Agency, and Disruptions: Confronting Modernity's Wager*. Eugene, OR: Cascade, 2020.

Brother John of Taizé. *Friends in Christ: Paths to New Understandings of Church*. Maryknoll, NY: Orbis, 2012.

Browning, Robert L., and Roy A. Reed. *The Sacraments in Religious Education and Liturgy: An Ecumenical Model*. Birmingham, AL: Religious Education, 1985.

Bruner, Frederick Dale. *Matthew: A Commentary—Volume 1: The Christbook, Matthew 1–12*. Rev. and Exp. ed. Grand Rapids: Eerdmans, 2004.

Calvin, John. *Commentaries on the Epistles of Paul to the Galatians and Ephesians*. Translated by William Pringle. Edinburgh: Calvin Translation Society, 1854.

Captari, Laura E., et al. "Prejudicial and Welcoming Attitudes toward Syrian Refugees: The Role of Cultural Humility and Moral Foundations." *Journal of Psychology and Theology* 47 (2007) 123–29.

Carmen, Peter J. B. "I Was a Stranger." *The Christian Century* (December 16, 2008) 12–13.

Carlson, Marianne M., et al. "We Welcome Refugees? Understanding the Relationship between Religious Orientation, Religious Commitment, Personality, and Prejudicial Attitudes toward Syrian Refugees." *International Journal for the Psychology of Religion* 29 (2019) 94–107.

Carvalhaes, Claudio. *Eucharist and Globalization: Redrawing the Borders of Eucharistic Hospitality*. Eugene, OR: Pickwick, 2013.

Chester, Tim. *Truth We Can Touch: How Baptism and Communion Shape our Lives*. Wheaton, IL: Crossway, 2020.

Chung, Jaeyeon Lucy. "Toward an Asian American Pastoral Theology of Radical Hospitality: Caring for Undocumented Migrants." *Journal of Pastoral Theology* 30 (2020) 121–35.

Clarke, Brian, and Stuart Macdonald. *Leaving Christianity: Changing Allegiances in Canada since 1945*. Montreal: McGill-Queen's University Press, 2017.

Collins, Helen. *Reordering Theological Reflection: Starting with Scripture*. London: SCM, 2020.

Cousins, Robert. "Blessed to Be a Blessing: A Missional Biblical Theology for Intercultural Ministry." In *From The Margins to the Centre: The Diaspora Effect*, edited by Michael Krause et al., 38–55. Toronto: Tyndale, 2018.

Craddock, Fred B. *Luke*. Interpretation: A Bible Commentary for Teaching and Preaching, Louisville: John Knox, 1917.

Deymaz, Mark. *Building a Healthy Multi-Ethnic Church: Mandate, Commitments, and Practices of a Diverse Congregation*. San Francisco: John Wiley & Sons, 2007.

Dixon, Jeffery C., and Michael S. Rosenbaum. "Nice to Know You? Testing Contact, Cultural and Group Threat Theories of Anti—Black and Anti—Hispanic Stereotypes." *Social Science Quarterly* 85 (2004) 257–80.

Eklund, Rebekah. *The Beatitudes through the Ages*. Grand Rapids: Eerdmans, 2021.

Farley, Edward. "Interpreting Situations: An Inquiry into the Nature of Practical Theology." In *Formation and Reflection: The Promise of Practical Theology*, edited by Lewis S. Mudge et al., 1–26. Minneapolis: Fortress, 2009.

Ferguson, Everett, ed. *Studies in Early Christianity*. New York: Garland, 1993.

Fetterman, David M. *Ethnography: Step by Step*. Los Angeles: Sage, 2010.

Fisher, J. D. C. *Christian Initiation: Baptism in the Medieval West—A Study in the Disintegration of the Primitive Rite of Initiation*. London: SPCK, 1965.

Garces-Foley, Kathleen. *Crossing the Ethnic Divide: The Multiethnic Church on a Mission*. Oxford: Oxford University Press, 2007.

———. "New Opportunities and New Values: The Emergence of the Multicultural Church." *The Annals of the American Academy of Political and Social Science* 612 (2007) 209–24.

George, Sam, and Miriam Adeney. *Refugee Diaspora: Missions amid the Greatest Humanitarian Crisis of our Times*. Pasadena, CA: William Carey, 2018.

Graham, Elaine, et al. *Theological Reflection Methods*. London: SCM, 2019.

Green, Michael. *Baptism: Its Purpose, Practice and Power*. Downers Grove, IL: InterVarsity, 1987.

Bibliography

Habig, Marion A. *St. Francis of Assisi: Writings and Early Biographies: English Omnibus for the Sources for the Life of St. Francis.* Chicago: Franciscan Herald, 1983.

Hartog, Paul A. "Abraham and the Rhetoric of Hospitality and Foreignness in Hebrews and 1 Clement." *Science et Esprit* 72 (2020) 281–96.

Hays, Richard B. *First Corinthians.* Interpretation: A Bible Commentary for Teaching and Preaching. Louisville: John Knox, 1997.

Hinton, Perry R. *The Perception of People: Integrating Cognition and Culture.* London: Routledge, 2015.

Hogg, Michael A. "Social Identity Theory." In *Contemporary Social Psychological Theories,* edited by Peter J. Burke, 111–36. Stanford, CA: Stanford Social Sciences, 2006.

Jabbour, Nabeel T. *The Crescent through the Eyes of the Cross.* Colorado Springs, CO: NavPress, 2008.

Jones, L. Gregory. "Eucharistic Hospitality: Welcoming the Stranger into the Household of God." *The Reformed Journal* 39 (1989) 12–17.

Kaehne, Peter von. "Iranian Diaspora Ministry." In *Scattered and Gathered: A Global Compendium of Diaspora Missiology,* edited by Sadiri Joy Tira et al., 441–46, Eugene, OR: Wipf & Stock, 2016.

Kaemingk, Matthew. *Christian Hospitality and Muslim Immigration in an Age of Fear.* Grand Rapids: Eerdmans, 2018.

Kim Sun, Hyung Jin. "A Mennonite Perspective of Hospitality in Times of Migrations." *Science et Esprit* 72 (2020) 297–309.

Langmead, Ross. "Refugees as Guests and Hosts." *Exchange* 43 (2014) 29–47.

Lee, Moses. "What John Calvin Taught (Me) about Refugees." *The Sola Network* (October 2019). No pages. Online: http://sola.network/article/john-calvin-refugees.html.

Little, Don. *Effective Discipling in Muslim Communities: Scripture, History and Seasoned Practices.* Downers Grove, IL: InterVarsity, 2015.

Love, Rick. *Muslims, Magic and the Kingdom of God: Church Planting among Folk Muslims.* Pasadena, CA: William Carey, 2000.

Mannik, Lynda, and Karen McGarry. *Practicing Ethnography: A Student Guide to Method and Methodology.* Toronto: University of Toronto Press, 2017.

Mason, Jennifer. *Qualitative Researching.* London: Sage, 2018.

McGowan, Andrew B. *Ancient Christian Worship: Early Church Practices in Social, Historical, and Theological Perspective.* Grand Rapids: Baker, 2014.

"McMaster Research Ethics Board (MREB)." *McMaster University.* Online: https://research.mcmaster.ca/home/support-for-researchers/ethics/mcmaster-research-ethics-board-mreb.

Bibliography

Menakem, Resmaa. *My Grandmother's Hands: Racialized Trauma and the Pathway to Mending our Hearts and Bodies.* Las Vegas, NV: Central Recovery, 2017.

Mischke, Werner. *The Global Gospel: Achieving Missional Impact in our Multicultural World.* Scotsdale, AZ: Mission ONE, 2015.

Moghaddam, Fathali M. *Multiculturalism and Intergroup Relations: Psychological Implications for Democracy in Global Context.* Washington, DC: APA, 2008.

Moschella, Mary Clark. "Ethnography," In *The Wiley Blackwell Companion to Practical Theology*, edited by Bonnie J. Miller-McLemore, 224–33. Chichester: John Wiley & Sons, 2014.

———. *Ethnography as a Pastoral Practice: An Introduction.* Cleveland, OH: Pilgrim, 2008.

Mounce, Robert H. *The Book of Revelation.* Rev. ed. New International Commentary on the New Testament. Grand Rapids: Eerdmans, 1977.

Niebuhr, H. Richard. *Christ and Culture.* New York: Harper & Row, 1951.

Nieman, James R. "Congregational Studies." In *The Wiley Blackwell Companion to Practical Theology*, edited by Bonnie J. Miller-McLemore, 133–42. Chichester: John Wiley & Sons, 2014.

Nouwen, Henri J. M. *Reaching Out: The Three Movements of the Spiritual Life.* New York: Doubleday, 1986.

Oden, Amy G., ed. *And You Welcomed Me: A Sourcebook on Hospitality in Early Christianity.* Nashville: Abingdon 2001.

Oksnevad, Roy. *The Burden of Baggage: First Generation Issues in Coming to Christ.* Littleton, CO: William Carey, 2019.

Ortiz, Michelle, and Jake Harwood. "A Social Cognitive Theory Approach to the Effects of Mediated Intergroup Contact on Intergroup Attitudes." *Journal of Broadcasting and Electronic Media* 51 (2007) 615–31.

Payne, J. D. *Strangers Next Door: Immigration, Migration and Mission.* Downers Grove, IL: InterVarsity, 2012.

Pohl, Christine. *Making Room: Recovering Hospitality as a Christian Tradition.* Grand Rapids: Eerdmans, 1999.

Porter, Stanley E., and Anthony R. Cross, eds. *Baptism, the New Testament and the Church: Historical and Contemporary Studies in Honour of R. E. O White.* Sheffield: Sheffield Academic, 1999.

Pullenayegem, Chris. "Surviving or Thriving? —Principles for a Church That Is Becoming." In *From the Margins to the Centre: The Diaspora Effect*, edited by Michael Krause et al., 181–90. Toronto: Tyndale, 2018.

Rah, Soong-Chan. *The Next Evangelicalism: Freeing the Church from Western Cultural Captivity.* Downers Grove, IL: InterVarsity, 2009.

Riley, Hugh M. *Christian Initiation: A Comparative Study of the Interpretation of the Baptismal Liturgy in the Mystagogical Writings of Cyril of Jerusalem,*

Bibliography

John Chrysostom, Theodore of Mopsuestia, and Ambrose of Milan. Washington, DC: Catholic University of America, 1974.

Rønsdal, Kaia S. "We Were Invited to Friendships: Lived Hospitality." *Approaching Religion* 10 (2020) 20–36.

Roxburgh, Alan J. *Missional: Joining God in the Neighborhood.* Grand Rapids: Baker, 2011.

Saldana, Johnny. *The Coding Manual for Qualitative Researchers.* Los Angeles: Sage, 2021.

Scharen, Christian, and Aana Marie Vigen. "Preface: Blurring Boundaries." In *Ethnography as Christian Theology and Ethics,* edited by Christian Scharen and Aana Marie Vigen, xvii–xxviii. London: Continuum, 2011.

Schreiter, Robert J. "Theology in the Congregation: Discovering and Doing." In *Studying Congregations: A New Handbook,* edited by Nancy T. Ammerman et al., 23–39. Nashville: Abingdon, 1998.

Shipani, Daniel S. "Case Study Method." In *The Wiley Blackwell Companion to Practical Theology,* edited by Bonnie J. Miller-McLemore, 91–101. Chichester: John Wiley & Sons, 2014.

Siddiqui, Mona. *Hospitality and Islam: Welcoming in God's Name.* London: Yale, 2015.

Smith, James K. A. *Desiring the Kingdom: Worship, Worldview, and Cultural Formation.* Grand Rapids: Baker, 2009.

———. *Imagining the Kingdom: How Worship Works.* Grand Rapids: Baker, 2013.

Spoto, Donald. *Reluctant Saint: The Life of Francis of Assisi.* New York: Penguin, 2003.

Spradley, James P. *The Ethnographic Interview.* Long Grove, IL: Waveland, 1979.

Swinton, John, and Harriet Mowat. *Practical Theology and Qualitative Research.* London: SCM, 2006.

Tajfel, Henri. *Human Groups and Social Categories: Studies in Social Psychology.* Cambridge: Cambridge University Press, 1981.

Thurian, Max, and Geoffrey Wainwright, eds. *Baptism and Eucharist: Ecumenical Convergence in Celebration.* Grand Rapids: Eerdmans, 1983.

Trousdale, Jerry. *Miraculous Movements.* Nashville: Thomas Nelson, 2012.

Van Opstal, Sandra Maria. *The Next Worship: Glorifying God in a Diverse World.* Downers Grove, IL: InterVarsity, 2016.

Vander Zee, Leonard J. *Christ, Baptism and the Lord's Supper: Recovering the Sacraments for Evangelical Worship.* Downers Grove, IL: InterVarsity, 2004.

Vezzali, Loris, and Sofia Stathi. "The Extended Intergroup Contact Hypothesis: State of the Art and Future Developments." In *Intergroup*

Bibliography

Contact Theory: Recent Developments and Future Directions, edited by Loris Vezzali and Sofia Stathi, 114–30, London: Routledge, 2017.

———. "The Present and the Future of the Contact Hypothesis and the Need for Integrating Research Fields." In *Intergroup Contact Theory: Recent Developments and Future Directions*, edited by Loris Vezzali and Sofia Stathi, 1–7, London: Routledge, 2017.

Volf, Miroslav. *Exclusion and Embrace: A Theological Exploration of Identity, Otherness, and Reconciliation*. Nashville: Abingdon, 1996.

Wainwright, Geoffrey. *Christian Initiation*. London: Lutterworth, 1969.

Ward, Pete. *Introducing Practical Theology: Mission, Ministry, and the Life of the Church*. Grand Rapids: Baker Academic, 2017.

Webb, Alan L. *So You Want to Do a Qualitative Dissertation? A Step-by-Step Guide*. Scotts Valley, CA: CreateSpace, 2016.

Westrate, Cassie. "This is our Church." *The Banner* (May 13, 2020). No pages. Online: https://banner.org/our-shared-ministry/2020/05/this-is-our-church.

Wise, Tim. *White like Me: Reflections on Race from a Privileged Son*. Rev. and Updated ed. Berkeley, CA: Soft Skull, 2011.

Wolcott, Harry F. *Ethnography: A Way of Seeing*. Lanham, MD: AltaMira, 2008.

Yong, Amos. *Hospitality and the Other: Pentecost, Christian Practices, and the Neighbor*. Maryknoll, NY: Orbis, 2008.

Index of Modern Authors

Abrams, Dominic, 49, 107
Adeney, Miriam, 3
Aldiabat, Khaldoun, 32, 78
Allport, Gordon W., 10, 45, 157
Almedingen, E. M., 25
Alvesson, Mats, 16
Ammerman, Nancy T., 43, 97–99, 138, 154

Ballard, Paul, 11, 113–15
Baucum, Tory K., 130
Bavinck, Herman, 126–29
Beach, Lee, 2
Berkhof, Louis, 11, 129
Bethune, Pierre-Francois de, 28, 120
Bibby, Reginald W., 2
Bock, Darrell L., 121
Branson, Mark L., 42, 114, 116, 138, 157
Brother John of Taizé, 37, 140–41
Browning, Robert L., 129, 134–35
Bruner, Frederick Dale, 131

Calvin, John, 11, 25
Captari, Laura E., 33, 48, 108, 151, 155
Carlson, Marianne M., 47–48
Carmen, Peter J. B., 33, 78, 80, 93
Carvalhaes, Claudio, 44, 132–33
Chester, Tim, 44
Chung, Jaeyeon Lucy, 27–28
Clarke, Brian, 2
Collins, Helen, 113
Cousins, Robert, 11, 26
Craddock, Fred B., 121

Deymaz, Mark, 38, 118

Dixon, Jeffery C., 48, 107

Eklund, Rebekah, 149

Farley, Edward, 112
Farnsley, Arthur E., 97
Fetterman, David M., 71–72
Fisher, J. D. C., 127

Garces-Foley, Kathleen, 41, 117
George, Sam, 3
Graham, Elaine, 113–14
Green, Michael, 128

Habig, Marion A., 24
Hartog, Paul A., 24
Harwood, Jake, 45–46, 60, 105, 155
Hays, Richard B., 119–20, 136
Hinton, Perry R., 9, 10, 49–50
Hogg, Michael A., 49–50, 107

Jabbour, Nabeel T., 36
Jones, L. Gregory, 134

Kaehne, Peter von, 43, 81, 83, 95, 124, 147
Kaemingk, Matthew, 29–31
Kim Sun, Hyung Jin, 29, 31, 122, 142

Langmead, Ross, 26–27, 40, 83, 149
Lee, Moses, 11, 25
Little, Don, 39–40, 125, 147–48
Love, Rick, 3

Macdonald, Stuart, 2
Mannik, Lynda, 56
Martinez, Juan F., 42

Index of Modern Authors

Mason, Jennifer, 55
McGarry, Karen, 56
Menakem, Resmaa, 35, 146
Mischke, Werner, 35–36, 43, 145–46
Moghaddam, Fathali M., 50–51, 155
Moschella, Mary Clark, 7–8, 15, 17, 53, 56–60, 62–63, 66–69
Mounce, Robert H., 42
Mowat, Harriet, 6–7, 16, 54–55, 112

Niebuhr, H. Richard, 11, 26
Nieman, James, R., 7, 16
Nouwen, Henri J. M., 28–29, 120–21

Oden, Amy G., 22–23, 31
Oksnevad, Roy, 12, 34, 36, 39, 101–2, 145–49, 152
Ortiz, Michelle, 45–46, 60, 105, 155

Payne, J. D., 3
Pohl, Christine, 8, 11–12, 22–23, 25–26, 36–37, 60, 116, 122–24, 136–40, 142–45, 149–50
Pritchard, John, 10–11, 113–15
Pullenayegem, Chris, 40, 150–51

Rah, Soong-Chan, 23–24
Reed, Roy A., 129, 134–35
Rønsdal, Kaia S., 30–31, 151
Rosenbaum, Michael S., 48, 107
Roxburgh, Alan J., 3–4, 42, 114, 116, 138, 157

Saldana, Johnny, 54

Scharen, Christian, 13
Schreiter, Robert J., 114
Shipani, Daniel S., 15
Siddiqui, Mona, 38
Sköldberg, Kaj, 16
Smith, James K. A., 116–17, 129–30, 135
Spoto, Donald, 24
Spradley, James P., 8–9, 13–14, 19, 54–58, 63–64, 66, 70, 73, 165
Stathi, Sofia, 10, 46–47, 105, 155
Swinton, John, 6–7, 16, 54–55, 112

Tajfel, Henri, 10, 48–49, 156
Trousdale, Jerry, 39

Van Opstal, Sandra Maria, 12, 118, 123, 152
Vander Zee, Leonard J., 43–44, 128–30
Vezzali, Loris, 10, 46–47, 105, 155
Vigen, Aana Marie, 13
Volf, Miroslav, 12, 33–34, 40–41, 52, 131, 143–45, 151, 153, 156

Wainwright, Geoffrey, 127, 131
Ward, Pete, 6–7, 28–30, 112–13
Webb, Alan L., 55, 99
Westrate, Cassie, 6
Wise, Tim, 18
Wolcott, Harry F., 109

Yong, Amos, 12–13, 41, 119

Index of Ancient Sources

OLD TESTAMENT

Genesis

1:27	23, 154
18:1–15	29, 121

1 Kings

17:9–24	121

Psalms

9:9	27, 149
24	29

Isaiah

61:1–2	27

NEW TESTAMENT

Matthew

5:4	148–49
5:10	27, 149
13:30	129
25:31–46	22, 36
28	42

Mark

5:25–34	36
9:35	152

Luke

4:18–19	27
6:21	27, 149
10	42
10:5–6	116
24:13–35	29, 121

John

3:16	146
15	140
15:15	34

Acts

2:1–3	40

Romans

8:15	154
12:1–2	39, 147

1 Corinthians

11	126, 136
12:1	153
12:12–13	118–19

Galatians

1:2	124
3:28–29	25, 154

Ephesians

4:22–24	39, 147

Colossians

3:9–10	39

1 Thessalonians

5:18	123

1 Timothy

4:12	154

2 Timothy

1:13–14	124–25

Hebrews

13:2	121

Revelation

5:9	41
21	118, 123
22	118

EARLY CHRISTIAN WRITINGS

Ambrose

De Officiis Ministrorum	22

Francis

Regular non Bullata	24

John Chrysostom

Homiliae in Acta apostolorum 45	22, 23
Homiliae in epistulam ad Romanos 21	22–23
Homiliae in epistulam i ad Timotheum 14	23

www.ingramcontent.com/pod-product-compliance
Lightning Source LLC
Chambersburg PA
CBHW062044220426
43662CB00010B/1639